CONCEPTS AND CHALLENGES

MATTER

Leonard Bernstein ◆ Martin Schachter ◆ Alan Winkler ◆ Stanley Wolfe

Stanley Wolfe
Project Coordinator

GLOBE FEARON
Pearson Learning Group

The following people have contributed to the development of this product:

Art and Design: Evelyn Bauer, Susan Brorein, Tracey Gerber, Bernadette Hruby, Carol Marie Kiernan, Mindy Klarman, Judy Mahoney, Karen Mancinelli, Elbaliz Mendez, April Okano, Dan Thomas, Jennifer Visco

Editorial: Stephanie P. Cahill, Gina Dalessio, Nija Dixon, Martha Feehan, Theresa McCarthy, Maurice Sabean, Marilyn Sarch, Maury Solomon, Jeffrey Wickersty, Shirley C. White, S. Adrienn Vegh-Soti

Editorial Services: Thomas Daning, Richetta Lobban

Manufacturing: Mark Cirillo, Tom Dunne

Marketing: Douglas Falk, Maureen Christensen

Production: Irene Belinsky, Linda Bierniak, Carlos Blas, Karen Edmonds, Cheryl Golding, Leslie Greenberg, Roxanne Knoll, Susan Levine, Cynthia Lynch, Jennifer Murphy, Lisa Svoronos, Susan Tamm

Publishing Operations: Carolyn Coyle

Technology: Jessie Lin, Joanne Saito, Ellen Strain

About the Cover: Everything in the universe, regardless of its size, shape, color, or physical state, is made up of matter. The shiny matter shown in the larger photograph are gold bars. Gold is one of more than a hundred different elements. Each bar of gold is made up of countless identical gold atoms. These atoms are similar in many ways to the smaller image, which depicts a model of the atom.

ISBN: 0-13-024194-6

Printed in the United States of America

1 2 3 4 5 6 7 8 9 10 06 05 04 03

1-800-321-3106
www.pearsonlearning.com

Acknowledgments

Science Consultants

Jonathan Cohen
Science Teacher
Longfellow Arts and Technology
Magnet Middle School
Berkeley, California

Kenneth S. Fink
Liberty Science Center
Jersey City, New Jersey

Laboratory Consultants

Sean Devine
Science Teacher
Ridge High School
Basking Ridge, New Jersey

Vincent Dionisio
Science Teacher
Clifton High School
Clifton, New Jersey

Gregory Vogt, Ph.D.
Associate Professor, Civil Engineering
Colorado State University
Fort Collins, Colorado

Reading Consultant

Sharon Cook
Consultant
Leadership in Literacy

Internet Consultant

Janet M. Gaudino
Science Teacher
Montgomery Middle School
Skillman, New Jersey

ESL/ELL Consultant

Elizabeth Jimenez
Consultant
Pomona, California

Content Reviewers

Scott Denny (pp. 138,139)
Food Service Manager
Denville, New Jersey

Samuel P. Kounaves (Chs 4–6)
Professor of Chemistry
Tufts University
Medford, Massachusetts

Terry Moran (pp. 46 and 47)
Moran Research Service
Harvard, Massachusetts

George F. Palladino (Chs. 1 and 2)
Director, Master of Chemistry Education
Department of Chemistry
University of Pennsylvania
Philadelphia, Pennsylvania

Thomas Rauchfuss (Ch. 3)
School of Chemical Sciences
University of Illinois
Urbana, Illinois

Dr. Dirk Schulze-Makuch (pp. 24, 25, 98, 99)
Department of Geological Sciences
University of Texas at El Paso
El Paso, Texas

Todd Woerner (pp. 66 and 67)
Department of Chemistry
Duke University
Durham, North Carolina

Teacher Reviewers

Leonard GeRue
Hanshaw Middle School
Modesto, California

Charles Sehulster
Science Teacher
Horace Greeley High School
Chappaqua, New York

Contents

Scientific Skills and Investigations Handbooks

Chapter *1* Properties of Matter

Chapter *2* Density

Chapter *3* Elements and Atoms

Chapter **6** Suspensions

Appendices

Features

Hands-On Activities

How Do They Know That?

◈ Integrating the Sciences

Real-Life Science

People in Science

Science and Technology

INVESTIGATE

Web InfoSearch

What are scientific skills?

People are naturally curious. They want to understand the world around them. The field of science would probably not exist if it were not for human curiosity about the natural world.

People also want to be able to make good guesses about the future. They want to know how to use alternative forms of energy. They want to improve technology and communications.

Scientists use many skills to explore the world and gather information about it. These skills are called science process skills. Another name for them is science inquiry skills.

Science process skills allow you to think like a scientist. They help you identify problems and answer questions. Sometimes they help you solve problems. More often, they provide some possible answers and lead to more questions. In this book, you will use a variety of science process skills to understand the facts and theories in physical science.

Science process skills are not only used in science. You compare prices when you shop and you observe what happens to foods when you cook them. You predict what the weather will be by looking at the sky. In fact, science process skills are really everyday life skills that have been adapted for problem solving in science.

1 NAME: What is the name for the skills scientists use to solve problems?

▲ **Figure 1** Scientists use science process skills to understand what makes a nuclear power plant run safely, how robots work in spaces too small for humans, and why communications are better using fiber optics.

Contents

Observing and Comparing

Making Observations An important part of solving any problem is observing, or using your senses to find out what is going on around you. The five senses are sight, hearing, touch, smell, and taste. When you look at the properties of an ore or watch an ice cube melt, you are observing. When you observe, you pay close attention to everything that happens around you.

Scientists observe the world in ways that other scientists can repeat. This is a goal of scientific observation. It is expected that when a scientist has made an observation, other people will be able to make the same observation.

2 ▶ LIST: What are the five senses?

Comparing and Contrasting Part of observing is comparing and contrasting. When you compare data, you observe the characteristics of several things or events to see how they are alike. When you contrast data, you look for ways that similar things are different from one another.

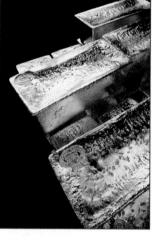

▲ **Figure 2** Silver and aluminum are alike in many ways. They also have many differences.

3 ▶ COMPARE/CONTRAST: How are a bar of aluminum and a bar of silver alike? How are they different?

Using Tools to Observe

Sometimes an object is too small or too distant to see with your eyes alone. Often, special tools are needed for making observations. Sometimes scientists use tools to make observations of things like radio waves or X-rays that are outside the range of our senses. Telescopes, spectrometers, microscopes, and magnifying glasses are all examples of tools that help with scientific observations.

▲ **Figure 3** Examining a slide with a magnifying glass

4 ▶ INFER: What are some things that scientists might need a microscope to see?

Hands-On Activity
MAKING OBSERVATIONS

You and a partner will need 2 shoeboxes with lids, 2 rubber bands, and several small objects.

1. Place several small objects into the shoebox. Do not let your partner see what you put into the shoebox.
2. Cover the shoebox with the lid. Put a rubber band around the shoebox to keep the lid on.
3. Exchange shoeboxes with your partner.
4. Gently shake, turn, and rattle the shoebox.
5. Try to describe what is in the shoebox without opening it. Write your descriptions on a sheet of paper.

Practicing Your Skills

6. **IDENTIFY:** What science process skill did you use?
7. **IDENTIFY:** Which of your senses was most important to you?
8. **ANALYZE:** Direct observation is seeing something with your eyes or hearing it with your ears. Indirect observation involves using a model or past experience to make a guess about something. Which kind of observation did you use?

2 Classifying Data

Key Term

data: information you collect when you observe something

Collecting and Classifying Data The information you collect when you observe something is called **data.** The data from an experiment or from observations you have made are first recorded, or written down. Then, they are classified.

When you classify data, you group things together based on how they are alike. This information often comes from making comparisons as you observe. You may classify by size, shape, color, use, or any other important feature. Classifying data helps you recognize and understand the relationships between things. Classification makes studying large groups of things easier. For example, physical scientists use classification to organize different types of elements.

5 EXPLAIN: How can you classify data?

Hands-On Activity

ORGANIZING LIQUIDS

You will need 10 to 15 jars or bottles filled with a variety of liquids.

1. Carefully examine the liquids in the containers. Observe their color, thickness, and composition. Notice what happens when you gently shake the bottle. What happens when you let the liquid settle?
2. Make a system for classifying the liquids.
3. Categorize all the liquids.
4. Write a description of how you would use your classification system to classify a new liquid that you have never seen before.

Practicing Your Skills

5. ANALYZE: How did you classify the liquids?
6. EXPLAIN: Why is a classification system useful?

3 Modeling and Simulating

Key Terms

model: tool scientists use to represent an object or process

simulation: computer model that usually shows a process

Modeling Sometimes things are too small to see with your eyes alone. Other times, an object is too large to see. You may need a model to help you examine the object. A **model** is a good way to show what a very small or a very large object looks like. A model can have more details than what may be seen with just your eyes. It can be used to represent a process or an object that is hard to explain with words. A model can be a three-dimensional picture, a drawing, a computer image, or a diagram.

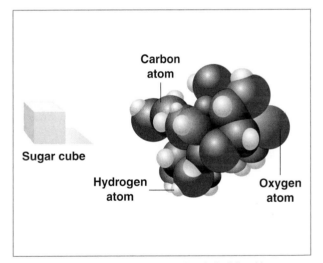

Sugar cube

Carbon atom

Hydrogen atom

Oxygen atom

▲ **Figure 4** Some schools have molecule-building kits. Each atom is color-coded according to the element it represents.

6 DEFINE: What is a model?

Simulating A **simulation** is a kind of model that shows a process. It is often done using a computer. You can use a simulation to predict the outcome of an experiment. Scientists use simulations to study everything from chemical reactions to the global climate.

7 DEFINE: What is a simulation?

4 Measuring

Key Terms

unit: amount used to measure something

meter: basic unit of length or distance

mass: amount of matter in something

gram: basic unit of mass

volume: amount of space an object takes up

liter: basic unit of liquid volume

meniscus: curve at the surface of a liquid in a thin tube

temperature: measure of the amount of heat energy something contains

Two Systems of Measurement When you measure, you compare an unknown value with a known value using standard units. A **unit** is an amount used to measure something. The metric system is an international system of measurement. Examples of metric units are the gram, the kilometer, and the liter. In the United States, the English system and the metric system are both used. Examples of units in the English system are the pound, the foot, and the gallon.

There is also a more modern form of the metric system called SI. The letters *SI* stand for the French words *Système International.* Many of the units in the SI are the same as those in the metric system.

The metric and SI systems are both based on units of ten. This makes them easy to use. Each unit in these systems is ten times greater than the unit before it. To show a change in the size of a unit, you add a prefix to the unit. The prefix tells you whether the unit is larger or smaller. For example, a centimeter is ten times bigger than a millimeter.

PREFIXES AND THEIR MEANINGS	
kilo-	one thousand (1,000)
hecto-	one hundred (100)
deca-	ten (10)
deci-	one-tenth (1/10)
centi-	one-hundredth (1/100)
milli-	one-thousandth (1/1,000)

◀ Figure 5

8 ▶ IDENTIFY: What are two measurement systems?

Units of Length Length is the distance from one point to another. In the metric system, the basic unit of length or distance is the **meter.** A meter is about the length from a doorknob to the floor. Longer distances, such as the distances between cities, are measured in kilometers. A kilometer is 1,000 meters. Centimeters and millimeters measure shorter distances. A centimeter is 1/100 of a meter. A millimeter is 1/1,000 of a meter. Figure 6 compares common units of length. It also shows the abbreviation for each unit.

SI/METRIC UNITS OF LENGTH	
1,000 millimeters (mm)	1 meter (m)
100 centimeters (cm)	1 meter
10 decimeters (dm)	1 meter
10 millimeters	1 centimeter
1,000 meters	1 kilometer (km)

▲ Figure 6

Length can be measured with a meter stick. A meter stick is 1m long and is divided into 100 equal lengths by numbered lines. The distance between each of these lines is equal to 1 cm. Each centimeter is divided into ten equal parts. Each one of these parts is equal to 1 mm.

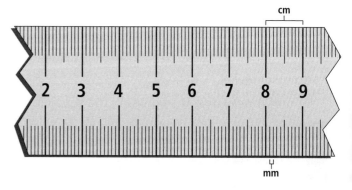

▲ **Figure 7** A meter stick is divided into centimeters and millimeters.

9 ▶ CALCULATE: How many centimeters are there in 3 m?

Measuring Area Do you know how people find the area of the floor of a room? They measure the length and the width of the room. Then, they multiply the two numbers. You can find the area of any rectangle by multiplying its length by its width. Area is expressed in square units, such as square meters (m^2) or square centimeters (cm^2).

Area = length × width

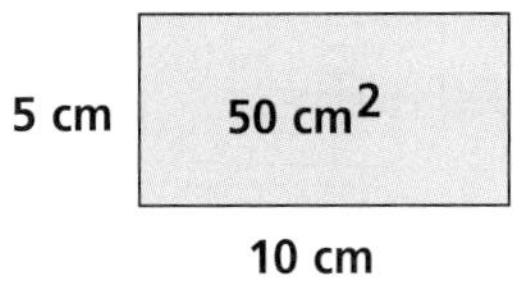

5 cm | 50 cm^2

10 cm

◀ **Figure 8** The area of a rectangle equals length times width.

10▶ CALCULATE: What is the area of a rectangle 12 cm by 6 cm?

Mass and Weight The amount of matter in something is its **mass.** The basic metric unit of mass is called a **gram (g).** A paper clip has about 1 g of mass. Mass is measured with an instrument called a balance. A balance works like a seesaw. It compares an unknown mass with a known mass.

One kind of balance that is commonly used to measure mass is a triple-beam balance. A triple-beam balance has a pan. The object being measured is placed on the pan. The balance also has three beams. Weights, called riders, are moved along each beam until the object on the pan is balanced. Each rider gives a reading in grams. The mass of the object is equal to the total readings of all three riders.

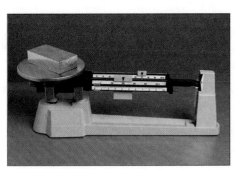

◀ **Figure 9** A triple-beam balance

Mass and weight are related; however, they are not the same. The weight of an object is a measure of Earth's pull of gravity between Earth and that object. Gravity is the force that pulls objects toward the center of Earth. The strength of the pull of gravity between two objects depends on the distance between the objects and how much mass they each contain. So, the weight of an object changes as its mass changes and as its distance from the center of Earth changes.

11▶ IDENTIFY: What instrument is used to measure mass?

Volume The amount of space an object takes up is its **volume.** You can measure the volume of liquids and solids. Liquid volume is usually measured in **liters.** Soft drinks in the United States often come in 2-liter bottles.

A graduated cylinder is used to measure liquid volume. Graduated cylinders are calibrated, or marked off, at regular intervals. Look at Figure 10. It shows a graduated cylinder. On this graduated cylinder, each small line is equal to 0.05 mL. The longer lines mark off every 0.25 mL up to 5.00 mL. However, every graduated cylinder is not marked in this manner. They come in different sizes up to 2,000 mL with different markings.

Always read the measurement at eye level. If you are using a glass graduated cylinder, you will need to read the mark on the graduated cylinder closest to the bottom of the meniscus. A **meniscus** is the curve at the surface of a liquid in a thin tube. A plastic graduated cylinder does not show a meniscus.

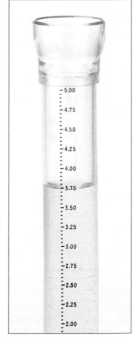

▲ **Figure 10** This glass graduated cylinder shows a meniscus.

The volume of solid objects is often measured in cubic centimeters. One cubic centimeter equals 1 mL.

Look at Figure 11. Each side of the cube is 1 cm long. The volume of the cube is 1 cubic centimeter (1 cm³). Now, look at the drawing of the box in Figure 12. Its length is 3 cm. Its width is 2 cm. Its height is 2 cm. The volume of the box can be found by multiplying length by width by height. In this case, volume equals 3 × 2 × 2. Therefore, the volume of the box is 12 cm³.

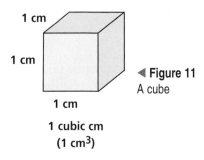

1 cm
1 cm
1 cm

◀ **Figure 11**
A cube

1 cubic cm
(1 cm³)

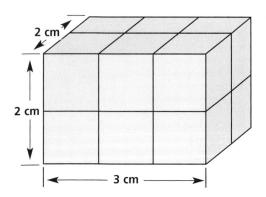

2 cm
2 cm
3 cm

▲ **Figure 12** The volume of a box equals length times width times height.

$$V = l \times w \times h$$

If you have a box that is 10 cm on each side, its volume would be 1,000 cm³. A liter is the same as 1,000 cm³. One liter of liquid will fill the box exactly.

12▸ CALCULATE: How many milliliters of water would fill a 12-cm³ box?

Hands-On Activity

CALCULATING AREA AND VOLUME

You will need 3 boxes of different sizes, paper, and a metric ruler.

1. Measure the length, width, and height of each box in centimeters. Record each measurement in your notes.

2. Calculate the volume of each box. Record each volume in your notes.

3. Find the surface area of each box. Record each area in your notes.

Practicing Your Skills

4. **ANALYZE:** Which of the three boxes has the largest volume?

5. **CALCULATE:** How many milliliters of liquid would fill each box?

6. **ANALYZE:** What is the surface area of the largest box?

Temperature **Temperature** is a measure of the amount of heat energy something contains. An instrument that measures temperature is called a thermometer.

Most thermometers are glass tubes. At the bottom of the tube is a wider part, called the bulb. The bulb is filled with liquid. Liquids that are often used include mercury, colored alcohol, or colored water. When heat is added, the liquid expands, or gets larger. It rises in the glass tube. When heat is taken away, the liquid contracts, or gets smaller. The liquid falls in the tube. On the side of the tube is a series of marks. You read the temperature by looking at the mark on the tube where the liquid stops.

Temperature can be measured on three different scales. These scales are the Fahrenheit (F) scale, the Celsius (C) scale, and the Kelvin (K) scale. The Fahrenheit scale is part of the English system of measurement. The Celsius scale is usually used in science. Almost all scientists, even in the United States, use the Celsius scale. Each unit on the Celsius scale is a degree Celsius (°C). The degree Celsius is the metric unit of temperature. Water freezes at 0°C. It boils at 100°C.

Scientists working with very low temperatures use the Kelvin scale. The Kelvin scale is part of the SI measurement system. It begins at absolute zero, or 0K. This number indicates, in theory at least, a total lack of heat.

COMPARING TEMPERATURE SCALES			
	Kelvin	Fahrenheit	Celsius
Boiling point of water	373K	212°F	100°C
Human body temperature	310K	98.6°F	37°C
Freezing point of water	273K	32°F	0°C
Absolute zero	0K	−459.67°F	−273.15°C

▲ **Figure 13**

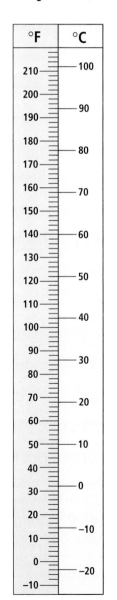

◀ **Figure 14** The Fahrenheit and Celsius scales

Hands-On Activity

READING A THERMOMETER

You will need safety goggles, a lab apron, 2 beakers, a heat source, ice water, a wax pencil, a ruler, and a standard Celsius thermometer.

1. Boil some water in a beaker.
   ⚠ CAUTION: Be very careful when working with heat. Place your thermometer in the beaker. Do not let the thermometer touch the sides or bottom of the beaker. Wait until the mercury rises as far as it will go. Record the temperature.

2. Fill a beaker with ice water. Place the unmarked thermometer into this beaker. Wait until the mercury goes as low as it will go. Record the temperature.

▲ **STEP 1** Record the temperature of the boiling water.

Practicing Your Skills

3. IDENTIFY: What is the temperature at which the mercury rose as high as it would go?

4. IDENTIFY: What is the temperature at which the mercury went as low as it would go?

13▶ NAME: What are the three scales used to measure temperature?

5 Analyzing Data and Communicating Results

Key Term

communication: sharing information

Analyzing Data When you organize information, you put it in a logical order. In scientific experiments, it is important to organize your data. Data collected during an experiment are not very useful unless they are organized and easy to read. It is also important to organize your data if you plan to share the results of your experiment.

Scientists often organize information visually by using data tables, charts, graphs, and diagrams. By using tables, charts, graphs, and diagrams, scientists can display a lot of information in a small space. They also make it easier to compare and interpret data.

Tables are made up of rows and columns. Columns run up and down. Rows run from left to right. Tables display data in an orderly arrangement, often numerically. For example, reading a table containing the uses of sulfuric acid shows that the largest use of sulfuric acid is in fertilizers. Figure 15 is a table that shows some uses of sulfuric acid.

USES OF SULFURIC ACID	
Product	Percentage
Dyes, batteries, paint, explosives	15
Raw materials	15
Fertilizers	60
Petroleum refining	5
Metal processing	5

▲ Figure 15

Graphs, such as bar graphs, line graphs, and circle graphs, often use special coloring, shading, or patterns to represent information. Keys indicate what the special markings represent. Line graphs have horizontal (*x*) and vertical (*y*) axes to indicate such things as time and quantities.

▶ 14 **EXPLAIN:** How do tables and graphs help you analyze data?

Sharing Results When you talk to a friend, you are communicating, or sharing information. If you write a letter or a report, you are also communicating but in a different way. Scientists communicate all the time. They communicate to share results, information, and opinions. They write books and magazine or newspaper articles. They may also create Web sites about their work. This is called written **communication.**

Graphs are a visual way to communicate. The circle graph in Figure 16 is showing the same information that is shown in Figure 15. The circle graph presents the information in a different way.

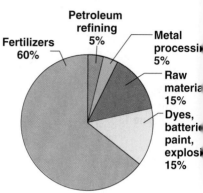

▲ **Figure 16** Circle graphs are a good way to show parts of a whole.

▶ 15 **LIST:** What are some ways to communicate the results of an experiment?

6 Making Predictions

Key Terms

infer: to form a conclusion

predict: to state ahead of time what you think is going to happen

Thinking of Possibilities When you **infer** something, you form a conclusion. This is called making an inference. Your conclusion will usually be based on observations or past experience. You may use logic to form your statement. Your statement might be supported by evidence and perhaps can be tested by an experiment. An inference is not a fact. It is only one possible explanation.

When you **predict,** you state ahead of time what you think will happen. Predictions about future events are based on inferences, evidence, or past experience. The two science process skills of inferring and predicting are very closely related.

▶ 16 **CONTRAST:** What is the difference between inferring and predicting?

How do you conduct a scientific investigation?

By now, you should have a good understanding of the science process skills. These skills are used to solve many science problems. There is also a basic procedure, or plan, that scientists usually follow when conducting investigations. Some people call this procedure the scientific method.

The scientific method is a series of steps that can serve as a guide to solving problems or answering questions. It uses many of the science process skills you know, such as observing and predicting.

Not all experiments use all of the steps in the scientific method. Some experiments follow all of them, but in a different order. In fact, there is no one right scientific method. Each problem is different. Some problems may require steps that another problem would not. However, most investigations will follow the same basic procedure.

▶ 1 DESCRIBE: What is the scientific method?

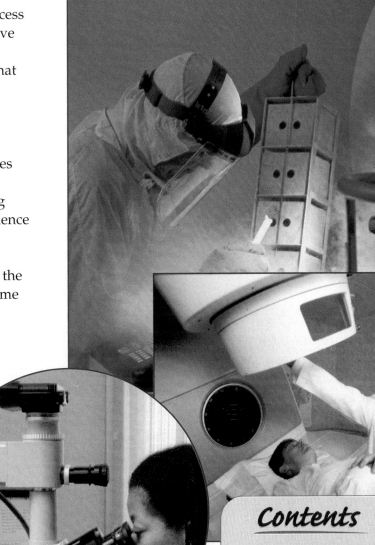

▲ **Figure 1** Scientists use the scientific method to guide experiments.

Contents

1 Identifying a Problem and Doing Research

2 Forming a Hypothesis

3 Designing and Carrying Out an Experiment

4 Recording and Analyzing Data

5 Stating a Conclusion

6 Writing a Report

1 Identifying a Problem and Doing Research

Starting an Investigation Scientists often state a problem as a question. This is the first step in a scientific investigation. Most experiments begin by asking a scientific question. That is, they ask a question that can be answered by gathering evidence. This question is the reason for the scientific investigation. It also helps determine how the investigation will proceed.

Have you ever done background research for a science project? When you do this kind of research, you are looking for data that others have already obtained on the same subject. You can gather research by reading books, magazines, and newspapers, and by using the Internet to find out what other scientists have done. Doing research is the first step of gathering evidence for a scientific investigation.

▶ **IDENTIFY:** What is the first step of a scientific investigation?

BUILDING SCIENCE SKILLS

Researching Background Information Suppose you notice that the brown paper towels at school do not seem to soak up as much water as the paper towels used in your home. You wonder which kinds of paper towels absorb, or soak up, the most water. You wonder if there is a connection between the paper towels' thickness and absorbency.

To determine which paper towels are most absorbent, look for information on paper towels in magazines, in books, or on the Internet. Put your findings in a report.

▲ **Figure 2** Testing paper towels for absorbency

2 Forming a Hypothesis

Key Terms

hypothesis: suggested answer to a question or problem

theory: set of hypotheses that have been supported by testing over and over again

Focusing the Investigation Scientists usually state clearly what they expect to find out in an investigation. This is called stating a hypothesis. A **hypothesis** is a suggested answer to a question or a solution to a problem. Stating a hypothesis helps to keep you focused on the problem and helps you decide what to test.

To form their hypotheses, scientists must think of possible explanations for a set of observations or they must suggest possible answers to a scientific question. One of those explanations becomes the hypothesis. In science, a hypothesis must include something that can be tested.

A hypothesis is more than just a guess. It must consider observations, past experiences, and previous knowledge. It is an inference turned into a statement that can be tested. A set of hypotheses that have been supported by testing over and over again by many scientists is called a **theory.** An example is the theory that explains how living things have evolved, or changed, over time.

A hypothesis can take the form of an "if . . . then" statement. A well-worded hypothesis is a guide for how to set up and perform an experiment.

▶ **DESCRIBE:** How does a scientist form a hypothesis?

BUILDING SCIENCE SKILLS

Developing a Hypothesis A hypothesis for an experiment about which paper towels absorb the most water might be stated as follows:

If thicker paper towels soak up more water than thin paper towels, then thickness is an important factor for paper towel absorbency.

However, what do you mean by thicker? Are the paper towels really different? Does color or design make a difference? You need to make your hypothesis specific. Revise the hypothesis above to make it more specific.

3 Designing and Carrying Out an Experiment

Key Terms

variable: anything that can affect the outcome of an experiment

constant: something that does not change

controlled experiment: experiment in which all the conditions except one are kept constant

Testing the Hypothesis Scientists need to plan how to test their hypotheses. This means they must design an experiment. The plan must be a step-by-step procedure. It should include a record of any observations made or measurements taken.

All experiments must take variables into account. A **variable** is anything that can affect the outcome of an experiment. Room temperature, amount of sunlight, and water vapor in the air are just some of the many variables that could affect the outcome of an experiment.

▶ **4 DEFINE:** What is a variable?

Controlling the Experiment One of the variables in an experiment should be what you are testing. This is what you will change during the experiment. All other variables need to remain the same. In this experiment, you will vary the type of paper towel.

A **constant** is something that does not change. If there are no constants in your experiment, you will not be sure why you got the results you did. An experiment in which all the conditions except one are kept constant is called a **controlled experiment.**

Some experiments have two setups. In one setup, called the control, nothing is changed. In the other setup, the variable being tested is changed. Later, the control group can be compared with the other group to provide useful data.

▶ **5 EXPLAIN:** Explain how a controlled experiment is set up.

Designing the Procedure Suppose you want to design an experiment to determine if a paper towel's thickness affects its absorbency. You decide to do a set of measurements to find out the absorbency of three kinds of paper towels in a controlled environment. You will measure the thickness of the paper towels and then determine how much water each paper towel soaks up to see if your hypothesis is correct.

In designing your experiment, you need to identify the variables. The three kinds of paper towels are all variables that could affect the outcome of your experiment. Everything about testing the effect of thickness on absorbency needs to be the same except the actual thickness of each paper towel.

Finally, you should decide on the data you will collect. How will you measure the thickness of the paper towels? In this case, you might want to record the thickness of each towel, its color, whether it absorbed water, and how much water was absorbed.

The hands-on activity on page 12 is one possible experiment you could have designed. It has one method for measuring the absorbency of the paper towels. Sometimes scientists try to measure the same thing two different ways to be sure the test is accurate. Can you think of another method to measure the absorbency of paper towels?

▶ **6 LIST:** How do constants and variables affect an experiment?

Hands-On Activity

CARRYING OUT AN EXPERIMENT

You will need 3 or more kinds of paper towels, a metric ruler, an eyedropper or pipette (preferably calibrated in millimeters), and water.

1. Get three different kinds of paper towels. To find the thickness of each kind of towel, measure the thickness of five towels and divide the result by five. Set up a data table for the information you gather.

2. Now you are ready to compare the absorbency of the paper towels. Cut the paper towels into squares of equal sizes. Squares that are 10 cm in size are good for testing.

3. Lay a square of paper towel on a tray or other nonabsorbent surface. Add drops of water one at a time until the paper towel has soaked up all the water it can. Record how much water was absorbed. If your eyedropper is not marked in milliliters, you can record your data in "drops." If it is marked, then you should record the milliliters.

4. Test all the paper towel samples the exact same way. Be sure that you only measure the water that is absorbed and that you let each paper towel sample soak up as much water as it will hold.

5. You are now ready to compare your data and see if they support your hypothesis.

Practicing Your Skills

6. **OBSERVE:** What happened in the experiment? How much water did each paper towel sample absorb?

7. **COMPARE:** Which paper towel absorbed the most?

8. **EXPLAIN:** What procedures did you follow to make sure the paper towels were all given a fair and equal test?

9. **IDENTIFY:** What is the variable being tested in this experiment?

4 Recording and Analyzing Data

Dealing With Data During an experiment, you must keep careful notes about what you observe. For example, you might need to note any special steps you took in setting up the experiment, exactly how you made the drops the same size each time, or the temperature of the water. This is important information that might affect your conclusion.

At the end of an experiment, you will need to study the data to find any patterns. Much of the data you will deal with is written text. You may read a report or a summary of an experiment. However, scientific information is often a set of numbers or facts presented in other, more visual ways. These visual presentations make the information more meaningful and easier to understand. Tables, charts, and graphs, for instance, help you understand a collection of facts on a topic.

After your data have been organized, you need to ask what the data show. Do they support your hypothesis? Do they show something wrong in your experiment? Do you need to gather more data by performing another experiment?

7 ▶ **LIST:** What are some ways to display data?

BUILDING SCIENCE SKILLS

Analyzing Data You made the following notes during your experiment. How would you display this information?

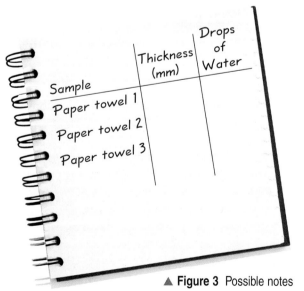

▲ **Figure 3** Possible notes

5 Stating a Conclusion

Drawing Conclusions A conclusion is a statement that sums up what you have learned from an experiment. When you draw a conclusion, you need to decide whether the data you collected supported your hypothesis. You may need to repeat an experiment several times before you can draw any conclusions from it. Conclusions often lead you to ask new questions and plan new experiments to answer them.

8 **EXPLAIN:** Why might it be necessary to repeat an experiment?

BUILDING SCIENCE SKILLS

Stating a Conclusion Review your hypothesis statement regarding the effect of the thickness of a paper towel on its absorbency. Then, review the data you obtained during your experiment.

- Was your hypothesis correct? Use your observations to support your answer.
- Which paper towel absorbed the most? Was it also the thickest?

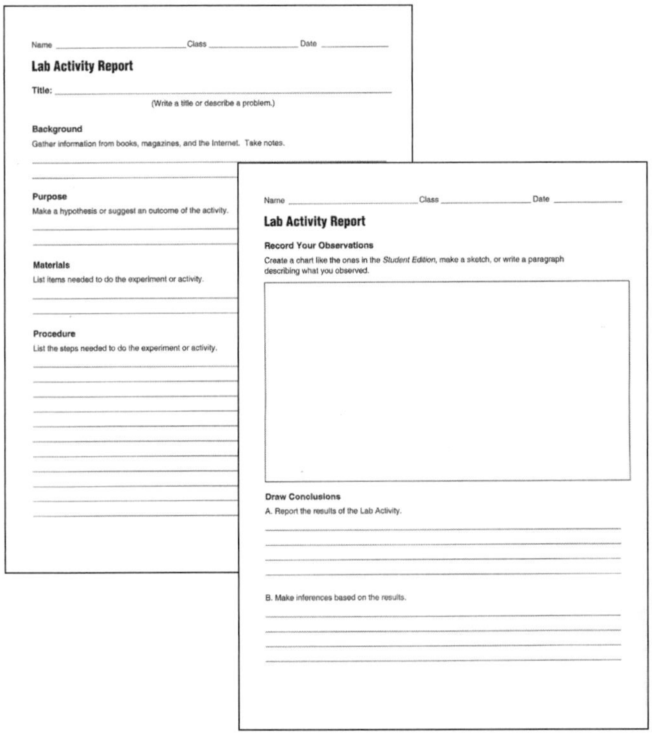
Name ______ Class ______ Date ______

Lab Activity Report

Title: ______

(Write a title or describe a problem.)

Background

Gather information from books, magazines, and the Internet. Take notes.

Purpose

Make a hypothesis or suggest an outcome of the activity.

Materials

List items needed to do the experiment or activity.

Procedure

List the steps needed to do the experiment or activity.

Name ______ Class ______ Date ______

Lab Activity Report

Record Your Observations

Create a chart like the ones in the *Student Edition*, make a sketch, or write a paragraph describing what you observed.

Draw Conclusions

A. Report the results of the Lab Activity.

B. Make inferences based on the results.

▲ **Figure 4** Throughout this program, you may use forms like these to organize your lab reports.

6 Writing a Report

Communicating Results Scientists keep careful written records of their observations and findings. These records are used to create a lab report. Lab reports are a form of written communication. They explain what happened in the experiment. A good lab report should be written so that anyone reading it can duplicate the experiment. It should contain the following information:

- A title
- A purpose
- Background information
- Your hypothesis
- Materials used
- Your step-by-step procedure
- Your observations
- Your recorded data
- Your analysis of the data
- Your conclusions

Your conclusions should relate back to the questions you asked in the "purpose" section of your report. Also, the report should not have any experimental errors that might have caused unexpected results. For example, did you follow the steps in the correct order? Did an unexpected variable interfere with your results? Was your equipment clean and in good working order? This explanation of possible errors should also be part of your conclusions.

9 **EXPLAIN:** Why is it important to explain possible errors in your lab report?

BUILDING SCIENCE SKILLS

Writing a Lab Report Write a lab report to communicate to other scientists your discoveries about the effect of a paper towel's thickness on its water absorbency. Your lab report should include a title, your hypothesis statement, a list of materials you used, the procedure, your observations, and your conclusions. Try to include one table of data in your report.

LAB SAFETY

Working in a science laboratory can be both exciting and meaningful. However, you must always be aware of safety precautions when carrying out experiments. There are a few basic rules that should be followed in any science laboratory:

- Read all instructions carefully before the start of an experiment. Follow all instructions exactly and in the correct order.

- Check your equipment to make sure it is clean and working properly.

- Never taste, smell, or touch any substance in the lab that you are not told to do so. Never eat or drink anything in the lab. Do not chew gum.

- Never work alone. Tell a teacher at once if an accident occurs.

Experiments that use chemicals or heat can be dangerous. The following list of rules and symbols will help you avoid accidents. There are also rules about what to do if an accident does occur. Here are some rules to remember when working in a lab:

 1. Do not use glass that is chipped or metal objects with broken edges. Do not try to clean up broken glassware yourself. Notify your teacher if a piece of glassware is broken.

 2. Do not use electrical cords with loose plugs or frayed ends. Do not let electrical cords cross in front of working areas. Do not use electrical equipment near water.

 3. Be very careful when using sharp objects such as scissors, knives, or tweezers. Always cut in a direction away from your body.

 4. Be careful when you are using a heat source. Use proper equipment, such as tongs or a ringstand, when handling hot objects.

 5. Confine loose clothing and hair when working with an open flame. Be sure you know the location of the nearest fire extinguisher. Never reach across an open flame.

 6. Be careful when working with poisonous or toxic substances. Never mix chemicals without directions from your teacher. Remove any long jewelry that might hang down and end up in chemicals. Avoid touching your eyes or mouth when working with these chemicals.

 7. Use extreme care when working with acids and bases. Never mix acids and bases without direction from your teacher. Never smell anything directly. Use caution when handling chemicals that produce fumes.

 8. Wear safety goggles, especially when working with an open flame, chemicals, and any liquids.

 9. Wear lab aprons when working with substances of any sort, especially chemicals.

 10. Use caution when handling or collecting plants. Some plants can be harmful if they are touched or eaten.

 11. Use caution when handling live animals. Some animals can injure you or spread disease. Handle all live animals as humanely as possible.

 12. Dispose of all equipment and materials properly. Keep your work area clean at all times.

 13. Always wash your hands thoroughly with soap and water after handling chemicals or live organisms.

 14. Follow the ⚠ **CAUTION** and safety symbols you see used throughout this book when doing labs or other activities.

▲ **Figure 1-1** Water can exist in any of three states on Earth.

All things are made of some kind of matter. On Earth, most matter exists in one of three states. Matter can change physically from one state to another or it can change chemically. Water is special. It can exist in all three states at the same time under ordinary conditions of temperature and pressure.

►Can you name the different states of matter by identifying them in Figure 1-1?

Contents

1-1 How do scientists study matter?

Objective

Identify and describe the ways scientists study matter.

Key Terms

chemistry (KEHM-ihs-tree): branch of science that deals with the study of the structure and the makeup of matter and the changes matter undergoes

physics: branch of science that deals with energy and matter and how they interact

specialization (spehsh-uh-lih-ZAY-shuhn): studying or working in one area of a subject

Studying Matter Everything in the universe is either matter or energy. In order to study matter, scientists must also know about energy. The study of matter, energy, and their interactions is called physical science.

Physical science has two main branches. Some physical scientists study the structure and makeup of matter and the changes it undergoes. This branch of study is called **chemistry.** Other scientists study the interactions between matter and energy. This branch is called **physics.**

 NAME: What are the two main branches of physical science?

Specialization A specialist is a person who studies or works in one particular area of a subject. Working in one area of a subject is called **specialization**. Some of the specialized fields in physical science are listed in Figure 1-2.

 DEFINE: What is a specialist?

Importance of Physical Science Why study physical science? Physical science is an important part of everyday life. It is difficult to think of anything that does not involve physical science and the discoveries of physical scientists. For example, each year seat belts save thousands of lives. Seat belt technology is based on the laws of motion.

Physical scientists have also discovered how to harness nuclear energy. Using nuclear energy has both problems and benefits. Physical scientists are constantly working to solve the problems related to nuclear energy. Their solutions may someday solve the world's energy problems. Physical scientists are also researching other forms of energy for power. Solar panels, wind farms, and fuel cells are some alternative sources of energy.

The discovery of new materials has resulted in the production of a variety of ceramic tiles, various glass products, and plastics. Our leisure time has benefited through cable and satellite dish TV, lasers, computers, holograms, and CD and DVD players. Cars and airplanes have been made safer and faster.

SOME SPECIALIZED FIELDS IN PHYSICAL SCIENCE

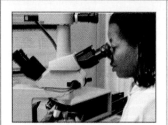

Biochemistry
Biochemists study the chemical substances occurring in living things. Some careers in biochemistry include medical research, plant and animal genetics, and pharmaceuticals.

Thermodynamics
Thermodynamics deals with heat and its conversion to other forms of energy. Research and engineering are two careers to pursue if you are interested in the study of thermodynamics.

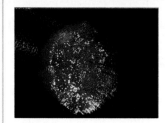

Optics
Optics is the science of light and vision. Some careers in the field of optics include optician and research scientist in such areas as lasers and optical fibers.

Nuclear Physics
Nuclear physicists study the characteristics, behavior, and structure of atomic nuclei. Careers include research, reactor manufacturing, and power plant operation.

▲ Figure 1-2

Studying matter and how it reacts with other substances has helped create all of these things.

 LIST: What are some of the products that have been created because of the work of physical scientists?

✓ CHECKING CONCEPTS

1. The two main branches of physical science are chemistry and _____.

2. Physical science is the study of matter and _____.

3. A person who works in only one area of a subject is a _____.

4. Physical scientists have helped develop ceramics, plastics, and _____.

5. The harnessing of _____ energy by physical scientists has helped reduce the world's energy problems.

 THINKING CRITICALLY

6. **ANALYZE:** Why do you think the number of specialized fields in physical science has grown during the past few decades?

7. **LIST:** What are three ways in which physical science is important in your daily life?

Web InfoSearch

A Career in Physical Science If you like science, you may be interested in a career in physical science. Choose a career from Figure 1-2, or a field of science that interests you.

SEARCH: Use the Internet to find out what education is required, what you will do on the job, and what tools you might need to perform this job. Write a short report about your results. Start your search at www.conceptsandchallenges.com. Some key search words are **biochemist** and **nuclear physicist.**

 People in Science

SCIENTIFIC ILLUSTRATOR

Do you like to draw? If so, you may be interested in a career as a scientific illustrator. You can see the work of scientific illustrators on many pages in this book. Scientific illustrators make drawings, diagrams, and sketches to illustrate scientific processes, structures, cycles, or equations, helping people to understand scientific concepts.

Scientific illustrators are employed by publishers of science books and journals or by advertisers. The drawings of scientific illustrators are used in sales brochures, advertisements, and even in this book. In the catalogs of scientific supply houses and pharmaceutical companies, many drawings are used to demonstrate equipment and other supplies.

▲ **Figure 1-3** Scientific illustrators often use computers as tools.

If you are interested in becoming a scientific illustrator, you need a college degree in graphics or fine arts. Many scientific illustrators also find a background in the sciences helpful in their careers.

Thinking Critically How does the work of a scientific illustrator help people learn science?

1-2 What are the properties of matter?

INVESTIGATE

Air as Matter
HANDS-ON ACTIVITY

1. Stuff a tissue into the bottom of a glass. Fill a pail with water.
2. Turn the glass upside down; push it straight down into the water.
3. Pull the glass straight out of the water and feel the tissue.
4. Record your observations.

THINK ABOUT IT: Did water enter the glass? How do you know? What does this tell you about air?

STEP 2

Objective
Identify two basic properties of matter.

Key Terms
matter: anything that has mass and takes up space

properties (PRAHP-uhr-teez): characteristics used to describe an object

Matter Look around you. What do all the objects you see around you have in common? They are all made up of matter. **Matter** is anything that has mass and takes up space. Mass is the amount of matter a sample of matter contains. The amount of space the sample takes up is its volume.

Water is matter. A glass filled with water is heavier than an empty glass. The water-filled glass is heavier because water has more mass than the air in the empty container. If you were to keep adding water to a filled glass, the water would overflow. It would overflow because water takes up space, leaving no room in the glass.

Air is matter, too. A balloon filled with air is heavier than a balloon that is not blown up because air has mass. When you blow air into a balloon, the balloon gets larger as air takes up space.

▶ DEFINE: What is matter?

Defining Properties How would you describe a hot-air balloon? You might say that it is rounded, blue, and striped. These are **properties** of that balloon. Properties are characteristics used to describe an object.

Not all hot-air balloons have the same properties. A different hot-air balloon may be rounded, green, and dotted. Some properties are not basic properties. They do not apply to all examples of the object. A basic property of all hot-air balloons is that they are balloons.

▲ **Figure 1-4** Hot-air balloons have properties that describe them.

▶ DEFINE: What is a property?

Properties of Matter Mass and volume are basic properties of all matter. Mass is a measure of the amount of matter in an object. Volume is a measure of how much space the object takes up. Mass is measured in kilograms. Volume is measured in cubic meters. A cubic meter is a cube that is one meter long on each side.

Weight and density are also properties that may be used to describe matter. Weight is a measure of the pull of gravity on a sample of matter. Density tells you how much matter is in a unit volume.

 LIST: What are the two basic properties of matter?

✔ CHECKING CONCEPTS

1. All the objects you see around you are made up of _____.
2. Matter is anything that has mass and takes up _____.

3. Mass is a basic _____ of matter.
4. Weight is a measure of the pull of _____ on an object.
5. The amount of space taken up by matter is its _____.

THINKING CRITICALLY

6. **INFER:** What is the difference between mass and weight?
7. **EXPLAIN:** Why do you think scientists can use the basic properties of matter to help identify an unknown substance?

BUILDING SCIENCE SKILLS

Observing Choose three objects in your home or classroom. Examine each carefully. List four properties of each and the senses you used to help describe each.

How Do They Know That?

MASS IS A PROPERTY OF MATTER

Chemists are scientists who study matter. Antoine Lavoisier (1743–1794) was a French chemist. He was educated as a lawyer. However, he loved chemistry. Antoine was helped in his work by his wife Marie Anne. Unlike most women of the day, Marie Anne had received an education in the arts and sciences. This enabled her to work side by side in the lab with her husband.

Before the work of the Lavoisiers, little was known about chemical reactions. For example, it was believed that there were only four elements. People also thought that chemical activities could create mass.

▲ **Figure 1-5** Marie Anne and Antoine Lavoisier working together

Marie Anne and Antoine showed that these ideas were not true. They explained that mass is not created or lost during a chemical reaction. Before an experiment, Antoine measured all of the materials going into the reaction. After the experiment, he measured the materials produced. He was the first scientist to realize that reactions began and ended with the same amount of mass. He wrote the Law of Conservation of Mass. It states that mass is neither created nor destroyed during a chemical change.

Thinking Critically The burning of wood is a chemical reaction. When wood burns, is mass destroyed?

1-3 What are the states of matter?

Objective
Identify and describe four states of matter.

Key Terms
state of matter: any of the four physical forms of matter

solid: state of matter with a definite shape and volume

liquid: state of matter with a definite volume but no definite shape

gas: state of matter that has no definite shape or volume

plasma (PLAZ-muh)**:** state of matter made up of electrically charged particles

States of Matter You cool drinks with solid ice cubes. You wash your hands in liquid water. Water that evaporates from puddles after a rainstorm has changed to a gas called water vapor. Ice, liquid water, and water vapor all are made up of particles of water. Different forms of the same substance are called states. A **state of matter** is any one of the four physical forms of matter. The three most familiar states of matter are solid, liquid, and gas. A fourth state, plasma, is found mainly in stars like our Sun.

▶ **IDENTIFY:** In how many states can matter exist?

Solids Most of the objects that surround you are made of solids. A **solid** is a state of matter that has a definite shape and volume. In a solid, particles of matter are tightly packed together. The particles cannot change position easily. They can only vibrate, or move back and forth in place.

2 DEFINE: What is a solid?

Liquids Milk is a liquid. A **liquid** has a definite volume but no definite shape. Liquids are able to change shape because the particles of a liquid can change position. They can slide past one another. If you pour a liter of milk into different containers, the milk always takes the shape of the container. However, the volume of the milk stays the same. You cannot make a liter of milk fit into a half-liter bottle.

3 EXPLAIN: Why can liquids change shape?

Gases A **gas** is a state of matter that has no definite shape or volume. A gas takes the shape of its container. For example, air can take the shape of a basketball, a football, or a bicycle tire. If you fill a balloon with air, the air completely fills the balloon. A container of gas is always completely full. The particles of a gas are in constant motion. They are much farther apart than the particles in solids or liquids. They can move freely to all parts of a container.

4 DEFINE: What is a gas?

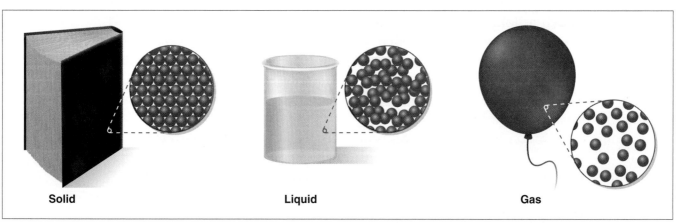

| Solid | Liquid | Gas |

▲ Figure 1-6 The three most common states of matter are solid, liquid, and gas.

Another State of Matter Matter can exist in a fourth state called **plasma**. Plasma is rare on Earth, but it is plentiful in other parts of the universe. Plasma has been found in stars, where the temperatures and pressures are very high. Matter in the plasma state is made up of small, electrically charged particles.

Scientists have been able to create plasmas in the laboratory. Such plasmas are relatively cool compared with natural plasmas. This plasma technology has been applied to many things you see everyday, such as flat-screen TVs, street lamps, and fluorescent tubes.

 DEFINE: What is plasma?

✓ CHECKING CONCEPTS

1. Plasma exists where _____ and pressure are very high.
2. In what state of matter can particles only vibrate in place?
3. What happens to the shape of a liquid when you pour it into a container?
4. What determines the volume of a gas?
5. What state of matter is air?

 THINKING CRITICALLY

6. **EXPLAIN:** What will happen to the particles of a gas if the gas is transferred from a small container to a much larger container?
7. **CLASSIFY:** Classify each of the following substances as a solid, a liquid, or a gas.
   - **a.** Cotton cloth
   - **b.** Rain
   - **c.** Carbon dioxide
   - **d.** Helium
   - **e.** Salt
   - **f.** Seltzer
   - **g.** Hydrogen
   - **h.** Sugar
   - **i.** Orange juice
   - **j.** Bricks

Web InfoSearch

Plasma As rare as plasma is on Earth, scientists have found ways to make use of it in some interesting ways.

SEARCH: Use the Internet to find out what kinds of products contain plasma. Then, create a chart. Next to each item on your list, include a picture of it. Start your search at www.conceptsandchallenges.com. Some key search words are **plasma** and **digital TV.**

 Integrating Earth Science

TOPIC: Earth's layers

EARTH'S MANTLE

The outer layer of Earth is called the crust. The crust is about 5 to 40 km thick, with the thickest part under the mountains. Beneath the crust is the mantle. The mantle is about 2,900 km thick. The upper part of the mantle is solid rock. Below the solid rock, the mantle rock behaves like a very thick liquid, such as molasses. This is because of very high pressure and temperatures. Like all liquids, this rock can flow. The rock also has some properties of a solid. It is in an in-between state of matter called the plastic state. A plastic material is neither a solid nor a liquid; it has properties of both.

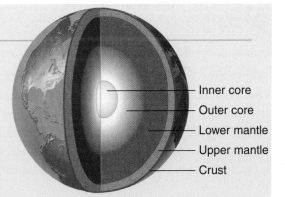

▲ **Figure 1-7** Earth's interior

Inner core
Outer core
Lower mantle
Upper mantle
Crust

Scientists would like to learn more about the plastic material in the mantle. However, they have not been able to drill that far into Earth. What they know has been learned by studying shock waves from earthquakes. Someday, scientists hope to find a way to drill deep enough to reach the mantle. Then, they will be able to study the properties of plastic rock directly.

Thinking Critically What might scientists do with the information they get from the plastic rock?

1-4 How does matter change state?

Objective
Identify ways in which matter can change from one state to another.

Key Terms
freezing: change from a liquid to a solid

melting: change from a solid to a liquid

evaporation (ee-vap-uh-RAY-shuhn): change from a liquid to a gas at the surface of the liquid

condensation (kahn-dehn-SAY-shuhn): change from a gas to a liquid

sublimation: change from a solid directly to a gas

State Changes Matter can change from one state to another. For example, water can change from a solid to a liquid. A change in matter from one state to another is called a change of state. There are four main kinds of changes of state. During a change of state, there is a change in heat energy. A substance either gains or loses heat as it changes from one state to another.

▶ **DESCRIBE:** What is a change of state?

Freezing and Melting If you fill an ice cube tray with water and place it in the freezer, the water will change to ice. Water changing into ice is an example of freezing. **Freezing** is a change from a liquid to a solid. Freezing occurs when the temperature of a liquid reaches its freezing point. At its freezing point, a liquid loses enough heat to change to a solid.

▼ **Figure 1-8** Part of this frozen iceberg is melting into the ocean.

When the temperature rises above the freezing point of water, ice changes to a liquid. A change from solid to liquid is called **melting**. Melting occurs when a solid gains enough heat to change into a liquid.

▶ **EXPLAIN:** What causes a liquid to freeze?

Evaporation and Condensation Before you go to bed tonight, fill an open plastic container with water. Mark the level of the water. Place the container in a warm, dry place. When you get up tomorrow, see what has happened to the water level. You will find that some of the water has "disappeared." Particles at the surface of the water gained enough heat energy to change into the gas state. **Evaporation** is a change from a liquid to a gas at the surface of the liquid.

You probably have noticed drops of water on your bathroom mirror after taking a hot shower. Hot water from the shower causes the temperature in the bathroom to rise. Some water particles gain enough heat energy to change to water vapor. Water vapor is the gas state of water. Water vapor is invisible. As particles of water vapor hit the cool surface of a mirror, they lose heat energy and change back into liquid water. This process is called condensation. **Condensation** is a change from a gas to a liquid.

▶ **EXPLAIN:** What causes condensation?

Sublimation When you fill an ice cube tray with water and place it in the freezer, you have ice cubes in a few hours. If you leave the tray untouched in the freezer for several days, the ice cubes get smaller. This is due to a process called sublimation. **Sublimation** is the changing of a solid directly to a gas, without passing through a liquid state. The temperature at which a solid changes to a gas is its sublimation point. Some other solids that sublime are moth balls (naphthalene), dry ice (CO_2), and iodine.

▶ **DEFINE:** What is sublimation?

✓ CHECKING CONCEPTS

1. Melting is a change from a solid to a
   _____.

2. Water changing into ice is an example of
   _____.

3. A change in matter from one state to another
   is called _____.

4. A change from a liquid to a gas at the surface
   of the liquid is _____.

5. Water vapor changing to liquid water is an
   example of _____.

6. Dry ice turning into gas is an example of
   _____.

THINKING CRITICALLY

7. **INFER**: What happens to the particles of a
   liquid as the liquid freezes?

8. **INFER**: What happens to the particles of a
   liquid as the liquid evaporates?

9. **CLASSIFY**: Identify the change of state taking
   place in each of the following situations.
   a. Water droplets form on the inside of your
      window on a chilly winter night.
   b. A full perfume bottle left open for several
      days is now half empty.
   c. A block of baking chocolate is heated until
      it can be poured into a measuring cup.

DESIGNING AN EXPERIMENT

Design an experiment to solve the following problem.
Include a hypothesis, variables, a procedure, and a
type of data to study.

PROBLEM: How can you identify an unknown
material?

Real-Life Science

FOG MACHINES

Dry ice is frozen carbon dioxide, a gas found in
the air around us. It looks like regular ice, but it is
much colder. The temperature of dry ice is about
−78.5°C or −109.3°F. If dry ice comes in contact with
your skin, heat is removed from your body so fast
that your skin seems to burn! For this reason, dry ice
should only be handled with insulated gloves.

Frozen carbon dioxide is called dry ice because
it does not melt. It changes directly from a solid
to a gas. This process is called sublimation. If you
watch a piece of dry ice, it seems to slowly
disappear into thin air as it sublimes.

▲ **Figure 1-9** Dry ice subliming

When dry ice is placed in hot water, a fog made
of tiny water droplets is produced. Such fogs, produced by a fog machine, can lend
a dreamlike or eerie mood to the sets of stage plays, rock concerts, or movies. A dry
ice fog machine is made up of a water barrel, a heater, and a fan. Dry ice is placed
in a bucket with holes in it. When the bucket is lowered into the barrel of hot
water, fog is produced. The fan then blows the fog through the air. The production
of fog is stopped by removing the dry ice from the water barrel.

Thinking Critically Where does the water that makes up the fog come from?

THE Big IDEA

How are changes of state part of the water cycle?

The water cycle is Earth's water recycling program. The water inside your cells, in your bathtub, underground, and even in glaciers is all part of the water cycle. Water endlessly cycles all over Earth—from the oceans to the clouds; from rain or snow into the ground; from rivers and streams back to the sea.

Think about a molecule of water (H_2O) in a puddle. Light from the Sun hits the water molecule, giving it an energy boost. The water evaporates and the molecule joins other molecules as they move from the liquid state to the gas state. The molecules enter the atmosphere as water vapor. Soon the water vapor cools and loses energy, condensing back to the liquid state. The water molecule joins other water molecules to form tiny droplets or ice crystals that make up clouds. The droplets increase in size until they are pulled to Earth by gravity. That is when you see rain, snow, hail, or sleet. This is called precipitation. Precipitation takes many forms, depending on the weather conditions.

On Earth, about 97% of the water is in the oceans. So, most of the action in the water cycle is evaporation from and precipitation back into the oceans. Sometimes the water cycle carries water molecules on incredible journeys.

Look at the illustration on these two pages. Then, follow the directions in the Science Log to find out more about "the big idea." ◆

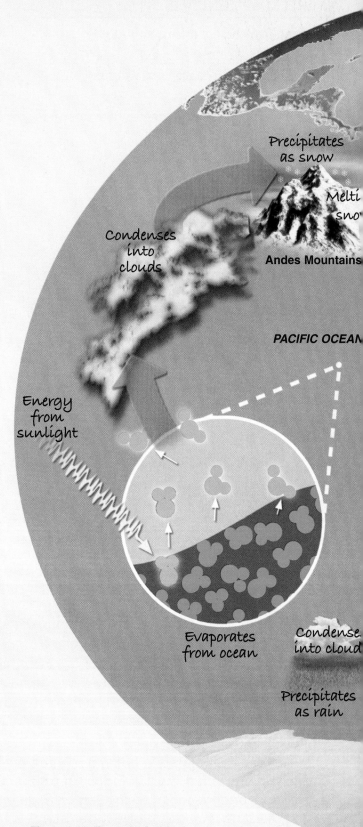

Precipitates as snow

Melti sno

Andes Mountains

Condenses into clouds

PACIFIC OCEAN

Energy from sunlight

Evaporates from ocean

Condense into cloud

Precipitates as rain

▲ **Figure 1-10** The path of a water molecule may be from ocean to ice cap and many places in between.

Evaporates
from
ocean

Amazon River

SOUTH AMERICA

Condenses
into clouds

ATLANTIC OCEAN

Precipitates as rain

Sublimes into
water vapor

Freezes
into ice

ANTARCTICA

WRITING ACTIVITY

Science Log

Track the path of a water molecule as it loops through the water cycle. Do this as if you are the molecule. Describe changes to your location and physical state. What happens when you change states? Describe what it is like to be solid, liquid, and gas. Start your project by visiting www.conceptsandchallenges.com.

A Journey of Water Molecules

Water evaporates from the Pacific Ocean. The water vapor blows over the Andes Mountains. It condenses into clouds and precipitates as snow. The snow melts and trickles down to a stream flowing into the mighty Amazon River.

Some of this water may become part of a cell in a rain-forest frog. The rest might flow all the way to the Atlantic Ocean. There, some of it evaporates and condenses again to fall as rain into the ocean.

Later, the ocean water travels to Antarctica and freezes in an ice cap. Some of the ice sublimes back into water vapor, and the cycle continues.

1-5 What are physical and chemical changes?

Objective
Distinguish between physical and chemical changes in matter.

Key Terms
physical change: change that does not produce new substances

chemical change: change that produces new substances

Physical Properties The states of matter are physical properties. Some other physical properties of matter include shape, size, color, and texture. Physical properties are characteristics that can be observed or measured without changing the makeup of a substance.

▶ **1** LIST: What are some physical properties of matter?

Physical Changes If you cut an apple in half and share it with a friend, it is still an apple. If you change water to ice, it is still water. If you crumple a sheet of paper into a ball, it is still paper. All of these changes are examples of physical changes. A **physical change** does not produce new substances.

▲ **Figure 1-11** The sawing of wood is a physical change. The burning of wood is a chemical change.

A physical change involves the physical properties of a material. Cutting an apple in half changes its size. Freezing liquid water changes its state. Crumpling up a sheet of paper changes its size and shape.

▶ **2** DEFINE: What is a physical change?

Chemical Changes If you take a crumpled sheet of paper and smooth it out, you can still write on it. It is still paper. Now, suppose you burn a sheet of paper. When substances burn, they combine with oxygen. Burning is an example of a chemical change. A **chemical change** results in new kinds of matter being formed. When paper burns, ashes, soot, heat, light, and gases are produced. You no longer have paper. Some other examples of chemical changes include the rusting of iron, the digestion of food, and the burning of gasoline in a car engine.

▲ **Figure 1-12** Rusting is an example of a chemical change.

▶ **3** CONTRAST: How is a chemical change different from a physical change?

✔ CHECKING CONCEPTS

Complete each sentence with the word **physical** *or* **chemical**.

1. Volume and color are examples of _____ properties of matter.
2. State is a _____ property of matter.
3. Changing water to ice is an example of a _____ change.
4. New substances are produced by a _____ change.
5. Iron rusting is an example of a _____ change.
6. Color and shape are _____ properties.

THINKING CRITICALLY

7. **ANALYZE:** Describe the changes that take place when a match burns. Are these changes physical or chemical?

8. **INTERPRET:** Mixing vinegar with baking soda produces carbon dioxide and water. Is this a physical change or a chemical change? How do you know?

9. **HYPOTHESIZE:** You find small pieces of ice instead of ice cubes in the freezer. State how this is possible.

BUILDING SCIENCE SKILLS

Classifying Classify each of the following examples as a physical change or a chemical change. Explain your answers.

a. Match burns
b. Glass breaks
c. Rubber band is stretched
d. Iron rusts
e. Ice melts
f. Sugar cube is crushed

Hands-On Activity

OBSERVING PHYSICAL CHANGES

You will need a bottle or jar with a narrow neck, ice cubes, and hot water.

1. Put a small amount of hot water into a bottle or jar. Place an ice cube over the opening of the bottle so that the ice cube will not fall in.
2. Observe what you see coming from the surface of the hot water.
3. Observe the bottle for a few minutes and note what you see happening near the top of the bottle.
4. Watch for another minute or two. Note if you see anything fall from the top of the bottle.

▲ **STEP 3** Observe the inside of the bottle.

Practicing Your Skills

5. **OBSERVE: a.** What did you observe coming from the surface of the hot water in Step 2? **b.** What caused this to happen?
6. **OBSERVE: a.** What did you see near the top of the bottle in Step 3? **b.** What caused this to happen?
7. **HYPOTHESIZE: a.** Did you see anything fall inside the bottle in Step 4? **b.** If so, explain what you saw and how it was produced.

LAB ACTIVITY
Observing Physical and Chemical Changes

Materials
Safety goggles
Lab apron
Modeling clay
Wax paper
Plastic teaspoon
2 Plastic cups
1 Antacid tablet
Tape measure
Cold water
Triple-beam balance

▲ **STEP 2** Measure the block of clay.

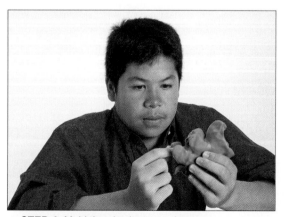

▲ **STEP 4** Mold the clay into any shape.

BACKGROUND

Physical and chemical changes occur everywhere around us. From a scientist's point of view, it is necessary to tell the difference between these two types of changes. A physical change involves a change in what you see, but it does not change the actual identity of the substance. A chemical change alters the identity of a substance and may involve a change in the way a substance looks as well.

PURPOSE

In this activity, you will observe and record data to decide whether the activity involves a physical or a chemical change.

PROCEDURE

1. Copy the chart in Figure 1-13. Put on safety goggles and a lab apron.

2. Take a block of modeling clay. Measure its dimensions using the tape measure. Record its mass using the triple-beam balance.

3. Shape the clay into a ball and record its mass. Measure the dimensions of the ball with the tape measure.

4. Mold the clay into a shape of your choice. Record its mass and try to measure its dimensions.

5. Put on safety goggles. Take the antacid tablet and place it in a small plastic cup. Measure 2 mL of water into another small plastic cup. Place both cups on the balance and record their combined masses.

6. Crush the antacid tablet and place it back it in the plastic cup. Place the cup with the crushed tablet and the cup with the water on the balance. Record their masses.

7. Pour the water into the cup with the crushed tablet. Record your observations. Place the cup with the water-tablet mixture and the empty cup on the balance and record their masses.

8. Clean up your area and dispose of the substances as directed by your teacher.

▲ **STEP 7** Pour the water into the cup.

Clay			Antacid Tablet	
Shape	Dimensions	Mass	Materials	Mass
Block			Tablet in cup and water in cup	
Ball			Crushed tablet in cup and water in cup	
Choice			Water in cup and empty cup	

▲ **Figure 1-13** Copy this chart and use it to record your observations.

CONCLUSIONS

1. **OBSERVE:** How is shaping clay an example of a physical change?

2. **ANALYZE:** Describe the changes that take place with the antacid tablet. Why does the mixture of the antacid tablet and water have a different mass after the reaction?

3. **INFER:** Based on your observations of the antacid tablet, what kind of change takes place when it is placed in water? Explain your reasoning.

4. **CLASSIFY:** Classify each of the following examples as a physical change or a chemical change. Explain your answers.
   a. cutting wood
   b. burning gasoline
   c. crumpling a sheet of paper
   d. wine turning into vinegar over time
   e. milk turning sour

Chapter 1 Challenges

Chapter Summary

Lesson 1-1
- Physical science has two main branches. They are physics and chemistry. **Chemistry** deals with the study of the structure and makeup of matter and the changes matter undergoes. **Physics** deals with the study of energy and matter and how they interact.

Lesson 1-2
- **Matter** is anything that has mass and takes up space.
- **Properties** are characteristics that describe an object. Mass, volume, weight, and density are four properties of matter.

Lesson 1-3
- A **state of matter** is a physical form of matter. A **solid** is a state of matter with a definite shape and volume.
- A **liquid** is a state of matter with a definite volume but no definite shape.
- A **gas** is a state of matter that has no definite shape or volume.
- **Plasma** is a fourth state of matter that is rare on Earth but plentiful in other parts of the universe.

Lesson 1-4
- Matter can change state.
- **Freezing** is a change from a liquid to a solid.
- **Melting** is a change from a solid to a liquid.
- **Evaporation** is a change from a liquid to a gas at the surface of the liquid.
- **Condensation** is a change from a gas to a liquid.
- **Sublimation** is a change from a solid to a gas.

Lesson 1-5
- Physical properties can be observed or measured without changing the makeup of a substance.
- A **physical change** does not produce any new substances. A **chemical change** produces new substances.

Key Term Challenges

chemical change (p. 26)
chemistry (p. 16)
condensation (p. 22)
evaporation (p. 22)
freezing (p. 22)
gas (p. 20)
liquid (p. 20)
matter (p. 18)
melting (p. 22)
physical change (p. 26)
physics (p. 16)
plasma (p. 20)
properties (p. 18)
solid (p. 20)
specialization (p. 16)
state of matter (p. 20)
sublimation (p. 22)

MATCHING Write the Key Term from above that best matches each description.

1. solid, liquid, or gas
2. study of the structure and makeup of matter and its changes
3. change from a gas to a liquid
4. change that does not produce a new substance
5. change from a solid to a liquid
6. state of matter that has no definite shape or volume
7. studying or working in only one area of a subject

FILL IN Write the Key Term from above that best completes each statement.

8. Water changing into ice is an example of _____.
9. During _____, liquids gain enough heat energy to change into the gas state.
10. A _____ is a state of matter with a definite shape and volume.
11. New substances are produced during a _____.
12. Anything that has mass and takes up space is _____.
13. Mass and volume are characteristics, or _____, of matter.
14. Milk is an example of a _____.
15. Two branches of physical science are chemistry and _____.

30 ◆ I

Content Challenges TEST PREP

MULTIPLE CHOICE **Write the letter of the term or phrase that best completes each statement.**

1. Water vapor changes to liquid water in a process called
   a. condensation.
   b. evaporation.
   c. melting.
   d. freezing.

2. The four states of matter are solid, liquid, gas, and
   a. metals.
   b. nonmetals.
   c. plasma.
   d. air.

3. Burning is an example of a
   a. state change.
   b. chemical change.
   c. physical change.
   d. physical property.

4. Particles of matter are tightly packed together in
   a. a solid.
   b. a liquid.
   c. a gas.
   d. a vapor.

5. Four properties of matter are mass, volume, weight, and
   a. distance.
   b. pressure.
   c. density.
   d. size.

6. Sublimation is a process in which a solid changes directly to a
   a. gas.
   b. liquid.
   c. ice.
   d. plasma.

7. Matter is anything that has mass and
   a. changes state.
   b. has color.
   c. takes up space.
   d. energy.

8. Evaporation is an example of a
   a. change of state.
   b. chemical change.
   c. solid changing to a gas.
   d. property of matter.

9. Matter that has no definite shape or volume is
   a. in the nonmetal state.
   b. in the gas state.
   c. in the liquid state.
   d. in the solid state.

10. Freezing is the opposite of
    a. evaporating.
    b. melting.
    c. condensing.
    d. solidifying.

TRUE/FALSE **Write *true* if the statement is true. If the statement is false, change the underlined term to make the statement true.**

11. <u>Weight</u> is a measure of the pull of gravity on an object.

12. When a solid melts, its particles <u>lose</u> heat energy.

13. The particles of a <u>liquid</u> can only vibrate in place.

14. <u>Physical properties</u> can be observed without changing the makeup of a substance.

15. All matter takes up space and has <u>color</u>.

16. Iron rusting is an example of a <u>physical</u> change.

Concept Challenges TEST PREP

WRITTEN RESPONSE Answer each of the following questions in complete sentences.

1. **COMPARE:** What are the differences between physical change and chemical change?
2. **DESCRIBE:** What happens to the particles of a substance as it changes from a solid to a liquid to a gas?
3. **INFER:** Why does evaporation require that heat energy be added to a substance?
4. **RELATE:** What is the relationship between the mass and the volume of an object?
5. **ANALYZE:** Is tearing paper a physical change or a chemical change?

INTERPRETING A DIAGRAM Match the picture of each object to the arrangement of its molecules.

6.

Solid

A.
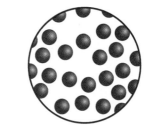

7.

Gas

B.

8.

Liquid

C.

▲ **Figure 2-1** A buoy floats in water.

Contents

What would happen if you were to drop an iron nail in the water next to the buoy in Figure 2-1? If you say that the nail would sink, you are correct. Yet, the buoy is also made of iron, and it is floating. Even the added mass of the animals on the buoy does not make it sink. It has to do with the density of the nail and the shape and density of the buoy. All matter has density. By making certain measurements, the density of any sample of matter can be calculated. Knowing the density of a substance can help us identify it.

►How is knowing density helpful in the science lab?

2-1 What is density?

Objective
Define density.

Key Term
density (DEHN-suh-tee): mass per unit volume

Density Which do you think is heavier, a kilogram of cotton or a kilogram of iron? You may already know the answer to this riddle. They both weigh the same amount. However, a kilogram of cotton takes up a greater amount of space, or volume. A kilogram of iron is small enough to hold in your hand. A kilogram of iron takes up less space because iron has a much greater density than cotton does. **Density** is the mass per unit volume of a substance. Substances that are very heavy for their volume are called dense substances.

▲ **Figure 2-2** The bale of cotton at the top has a mass of 1 kg. The iron frying pan below it also has a mass of 1 kg.

▶ **DEFINE:** What is density?

Units of Density You can find the density of a substance by finding the mass of a unit volume of the substance. Units of density include units of mass and volume. Mass is measured in grams. The volume of solids is measured in cubic centimeters. The volume of liquids can be measured in milliliters. One milliliter is equal to one cubic centimeter. Therefore, the density of any substance can be given in grams per cubic centimeter, or g/cm^3. For example, water has a density of $1 \ g/cm^3$. One gram of water takes up one cubic centimeter of space. The densities of some common substances are listed in Figure 2-3.

DENSITIES OF SOME COMMON SUBSTANCES	
Substance	**Density (g/cm³)**
Air	0.0013
Alcohol	0.8
Aluminum	2.7
Cork	0.2
Gold	19.3
Iron	7.9
Lead	11.3
Mercury	13.6
Silver	10.5
Steel	7.8
Water	1.0

▲ **Figure 2-3**

▶ **IDENTIFY:** In what units is density measured?

Using Density Density is a physical property of matter. Every kind of matter has a density that can be measured. The density of a pure substance is always the same. For example, the density of lead is always $11.3 \ g/cm^3$. The density of mercury is always $13.6 \ g/cm^3$. Density does not depend on the size or shape of the substance.

Density can be used to help identify different kinds of matter. Suppose two metals look similar. You know that one may be silver and the other aluminum. If you know the density of each sample, you can identify them. The sample with a density of $10.5 \ g/cm^3$ is silver. The sample with a density of $2.7 \ g/cm^3$ is aluminum.

▲ **Figure 2-4** Aluminum (left) and silver (right) look alike but have different densities.

 IDENTIFY: What kind of property is density?

✔ CHECKING CONCEPTS

1. Density is the _____ per unit volume of a substance.
2. When a substance has a high density, a large mass fits into a _____ volume.
3. The units of _____ are grams per cubic centimeter.
4. Density is a physical _____ of all matter.
5. The density of silver is always _____.

💡 THINKING CRITICALLY

6. **CALCULATE:** What is the density of a metal block that has a mass of 525 g and a volume of 50 cm^3?
7. **PREDICT:** How large a container would be needed to hold 800 g of water?
8. **SEQUENCE:** List the following substances in order from lowest density to highest density: iron, gold, steel, water, air, silver, and aluminum.

DESIGNING AN EXPERIMENT

Design an experiment to solve the following problem. Include a hypothesis, variables, a procedure, and a type of data to study.

PROBLEM: How can you determine the density of chalk?

◈ *Integrating Earth Science*

TOPICS: neutron stars, black holes

THE DENSEST OBJECTS IN THE UNIVERSE

What are the densest objects thought to exist? The answer is neutron stars and black holes. Here is how they form. A new star is made mostly of hydrogen. As millions of years pass, the hydrogen fuses and changes into helium. When the hydrogen is used up, the star becomes a red giant or a supergiant.

Supergiants start out with a much greater mass than the mass of our Sun. Such massive stars may blow up in a huge explosion called a supernova. After the explosion, some of the star's matter gets squeezed into a very dense object called a neutron star. The density of a neutron star is enormous. One teaspoon of matter from a neutron star would have a mass of 100 billion tons!

Some supergiants do not become neutron stars. The most massive stars collapse into black holes. A black hole has a density even greater than that of a neutron star. The density of a black hole behaves as if it is infinite. Not even light escapes the strong pull of gravity in a black hole.

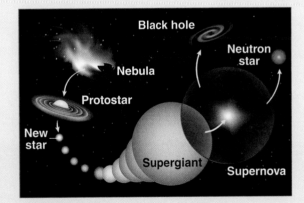

▲ **Figure 2-5** Stages in the life of a star

Thinking Critically Explain the meaning of the name "black hole."

2-2 How is density measured?

Objective

Explain how to find the density of a solid or a liquid.

Finding Density To find the density of a material, you must measure both mass and volume. You can find density by dividing the mass by the volume. Remember that mass is measured in grams. Volume is measured in cubic centimeters or milliliters, so density is expressed in grams per cubic centimeter or grams per milliliter.

▶ **1** **IDENTIFY:** What measurements must you make before you can calculate the density of a material?

Density of a Liquid You can find the density of a liquid using a graduated cylinder and a balance.

- Find the mass of the graduated cylinder. Record your measurement.

- Pour some of the liquid you want to measure into the graduated cylinder. Write down the volume of the liquid.

- Place the graduated cylinder with the liquid on the balance. Record the mass.

- Find the mass of the liquid by subtracting the mass of the empty graduated cylinder from the mass of the graduated cylinder with the liquid.

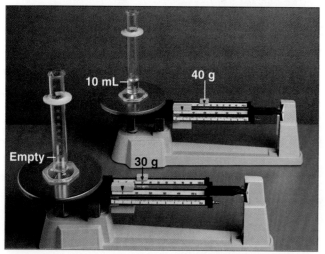

▲ **Figure 2-6** The empty graduated cylinder has a mass of 30 g. With the liquid the mass is 40 g, so the water has a mass of 10 g.

Now you are ready to calculate the density of the liquid. Look at the example shown. The mass of the liquid is 10 g. The volume is 10 mL. To find the liquid's density, divide its mass by its volume.

> density = mass ÷ volume
> density = 10 g ÷ 10 mL
> density = 1 g/mL

Notice that in this example, density is expressed in grams per milliliter. One milliliter is equal in volume to one cubic centimeter. The density of a liquid can be measured in grams per milliliter or grams per cubic centimeter.

▶ **2** **EXPLAIN:** Why can density be measured either in grams per cubic centimeter or in grams per milliliter?

Density of a Solid You can find the density of any solid if you know its mass and its volume. You can use a balance to find the mass of a solid. You can find the volume of a rectangular solid by multiplying its length by its width by its height. Look at the aluminum bar in Figure 2-7. Its mass is equal to 270 g. Its volume is equal to 10 cm × 5 cm × 2 cm, or 100 cm³. To find the density of the aluminum bar, divide its mass by its volume.

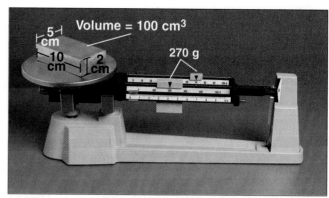

▲ **Figure 2-7** An aluminum bar of volume 100 cm³ has a mass of 270 g.

> density = mass ÷ volume
> density = 270 g ÷ 100 cm³
> density = 2.7 g/cm³

▶ **3** **DESCRIBE:** How can you find the volume of a rectangular solid?

✔ CHECKING CONCEPTS

1. What measurements must be known in order to find the density of a substance?

2. What are the units of density for a liquid?

3. What equipment do you need to find the density of a liquid?

4. What three measurements must you make when finding the density of a liquid?

5. How can you find the density of a solid with a regular shape?

💡 THINKING CRITICALLY

6. CALCULATE: If 5 mL of a liquid has a mass of 10 g, what is the density of the liquid?

7. EXPLAIN: When finding the density of a liquid, why must you first find the mass of the container holding the liquid?

BUILDING MATH SKILLS

Calculating Density Use Figure 2-8 to answer the following questions.

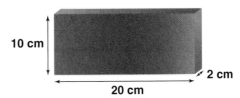

10 cm
20 cm
2 cm

▲ Figure 2-8

8. What is the volume of the bar?

9. If the bar has a mass of 500 g, what is its density? Show your work.

10. How would the density of the bar be different if its mass was 4,520 g? What would the bar be made of?

Hands-On Activity

COMPARING DENSITIES OF LIQUIDS

You will need a graduated cylinder, food coloring, water, corn syrup, vegetable oil, and glycerine.

1. Color the water and glycerine differently, so you can tell them apart.

2. One at a time, slowly pour about 10 mL each of the water, corn syrup, vegetable oil, and glycerine into the graduated cylinder.

3. Observe the liquids as they form separate layers.

4. Make a sketch showing the order in which the liquids have settled in the graduated cylinder.

▲ STEP 3 Observe how the liquids separate.

Practicing Your Skills

5. HYPOTHESIZE: Why do you think the liquids separate into layers?

6. INFER: Which liquid is the most dense? Which liquid is the least dense?

7. SEQUENCE: List the four liquids in order from least to most dense.

2-3 What is specific gravity?

Objective

Explain what is meant by specific gravity.

Key Terms

specific (spuh-SIF-ik) **gravity:** density of a substance compared with the density of water

hydrometer (hy-DRAHM-uht-uhr)**:** device used to measure specific gravity

Specific Gravity **Specific gravity** is the density of a substance compared with the density of water. It is often useful to compare the density of a substance with the density of water. Water is used as the standard for comparison because its density is 1 g/cm^3. You can find the specific gravity of a substance by dividing its density by the density of water.

Suppose you want to find the specific gravity of copper. The density of copper is 8.9 g/cm^3. The density of water is 1 g/cm^3. To find the specific gravity of copper, divide the density of copper by the density of water. The specific gravity of copper is 8.9. Notice that specific gravity has no units. When you divide like units, the units cancel each other out. The specific gravities of some common substances are listed in Figure 2-9.

SPECIFIC GRAVITIES	
Substance	**Specific Gravity**
Aluminum	2.7
Corn syrup	1.38
Diamond	3.5
Gasoline	0.7
Glycerine	1.26
Gold	19.3
Ice	0.92
Marble	2.7
Rubber	1.34
Water	1.00

▲ Figure 2-9

▶ DEFINE: What is specific gravity?

Measuring Specific Gravity The specific gravity of a liquid can be measured with a device called a **hydrometer**. When a hydrometer is placed in a liquid, it floats. The higher the specific gravity of a liquid, the higher the hydrometer will float. You can tell the specific gravity of the liquid by reading the marking at the surface of the liquid.

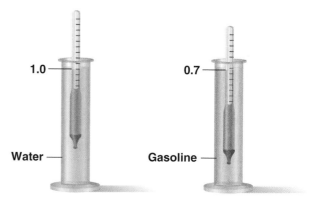

▲ **Figure 2-10** Water has a specific gravity of 1.00. Gasoline has a specific gravity of 0.7.

 EXPLAIN: What determines the height at which a hydrometer floats in a liquid?

Uses of Specific Gravity Specific gravity has many practical uses. It can be used to identify pure substances, because each substance has a particular specific gravity. Hydrometers are used in clinical laboratory tests to find the specific gravity of blood and of urine. Lab technicians look for signs of increased glucose (sugar) or protein. Dehydration, a loss of fluid in the system, is also detected by specific gravity.

▲ **Figure 2-11** A hydrometer can test the specific gravity of any liquid.

Specific gravity can also be used to check the chemical purity of substances. Industries use specific gravity to check the quality of many of their products. For example, specific gravity is used to check the amount of cane sugar in a solution. It also is used to check the purity of milk.

 NAME: What are some uses of specific gravity?

✓ CHECKING CONCEPTS

1. Specific gravity compares the density of a substance with the density of _____.

2. Specific gravity has no _____ because the density units cancel each other out.

3. A hydrometer is a device that can be used to measure the specific gravity of a _____.

4. The _____ at which the hydrometer floats depends on the specific gravity of the liquid.

5. The purity of milk can be checked by using _____.

💡 THINKING CRITICALLY

6. **PREDICT:** In which liquid would a hydrometer float lower, gasoline or corn syrup? Explain.

7. **CALCULATE:** Silver has a density of 10.5 g/cm^3. What is the specific gravity of silver?

8. **EXPLAIN:** Why does specific gravity have no units?

BUILDING SCIENCE SKILLS

Researching In a brief report, explain whether specific gravity could be useful in each of the following situations.

a. Determining the purity of vegetable oil

b. Determining whether a rock is real gold or fool's gold

c. Separating corn oil from corn syrup

d. Determining whether gasoline has been contaminated with water

---

 People in Science

MINERALOGIST

Minerals are natural substances found in soil and rock. Many products are made from minerals. For example, quartz is a mineral that is used to make timing devices in watches. Sulfur is a mineral that is used to make medicines.

Minerals must be mined, or taken from the earth. When a mineral deposit is found, a mining company needs to know how much of the mineral is present and what form the mineral is in. Mineralogists find answers to these questions. They take samples from a mineral deposit. They then study the specific gravity of the mineral to identify it and to determine its purity.

▲ **Figure 2-12** This mineralogist is studying a limestone deposit.

Mineralogists are employed by private industry, research laboratories, and the government. To be a mineralogist, a person needs a college degree. Many mineralogists also have advanced degrees. If you are interested in this career, you should have a good background in science and mathematics.

Thinking Critically For what part of this job would you need math skills?

2-4 What is displacement?

INVESTIGATE

Measuring Displacement
HANDS-ON ACTIVITY

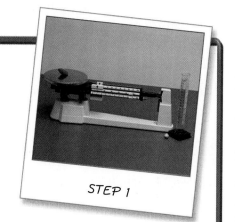
STEP 1

1. Use a balance to find the masses of a small stone and a marble. Record your measurements in a data table.
2. Fill a 100-mL graduated cylinder with water to the 50-mL mark.
3. Gently place the stone in the water. Notice how much the water level rises. This increase is equal to the volume of water displaced. Record the change in volume of the water in your data table.
4. Repeat Step 3 with the marble.

THINK ABOUT IT: What is the volume of the stone? Of the marble? Does the amount of water displaced by an object depend on its mass? How do you know?

Objectives

Define displacement. Find the volume of an irregular solid.

Key Term

displacement (dihs-PLAYS-muhnt): the replacement, or pushing aside, of a volume of water, or any fluid, by an object

Displacement About 2,000 years ago, a Greek scientist named Archimedes (ahr-kuh-MEE-deez) made an interesting observation. He stepped into a bathtub full of water and noticed that the water level rose. When he sat down, some of the water spilled over the edge of the tub.

What Archimedes observed occurs whenever an object is placed in water. When objects are placed in water, they make the water level rise. The water level rises because water is pushed out of the way by the object. This replacement of a volume of water by an object is called **displacement**.

▲ **Figure 2-13** Archimedes

▶ DEFINE: What is displacement?

Displacement and Volume When an object is placed completely under water, the volume of the water that the object displaces is equal to the volume of the object. Many objects, such as rocks, do not have a regular shape. You can use displacement to find the volume of an irregularly shaped object, as shown in Figure 2-14.

The stone displaces the water

▲ **Figure 2-14** When a stone is lowered into a can of water, it displaces a volume of water equal to its own volume.

A simple way to find the volume of an irregularly shaped object is to pour some water into a graduated cylinder or a beaker that is marked to show volume. Record the volume of the water. Then, carefully place the object in the container of water. Record the new reading. The volume of the object is equal to the difference in the two volume readings.

For example, if a rock displaces 5 mL of water, the volume of the rock is 5 mL. This is shown in Figure 2-15.

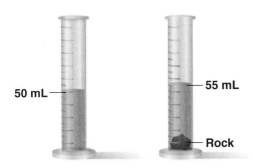

50 mL

55 mL

Rock

55 mL − 50 mL = 5 mL
Volume of rock = 5 mL

▲ **Figure 2-15** This rock displaced 5 mL of water. It has a volume of 5 mL.

 EXPLAIN: How can you find the volume of an irregularly shaped object?

✓ CHECKING CONCEPTS

1. If an object displaces 50 mL of water, the object's _____ is 50 mL.
2. When an object is placed in water, the water level _____.
3. The amount of water pushed aside by an object is called _____.

4. A rock is an _____ shaped object.
5. The _____ of an irregular object is equal to the volume of water it displaces.

THINKING CRITICALLY

6. **ANALYZE:** Does the amount of water displaced by an object depend on the object's mass? Explain your answer.
7. **EXPLAIN:** Why is displacement useful in finding the density of an irregularly shaped object?

BUILDING MATH SKILLS

Finding Volume Use displacement to find the volume of the following objects. Assume each has been placed in a graduated cylinder containing 50 mL of water.

a. A marble: new reading, 54 mL
b. A lead weight: new reading, 71 mL
c. A paper clip: new reading, 50.5 mL

 Real-Life Science

PREVENTING SPILL-OVER

Have you ever made an ice cream soda? Did some, if not most, of the liquid wind up on the table after you put in the ice cream?

What happens when you fill a glass with a beverage, then try to put ice in the glass?

In order to prevent this displacement and the mess it causes, you must first place the ice in the glass, then add the liquid. This prevents spill-over.

In the bathroom, both the sink and tub have a feature built in to prevent accidental overflow. Do you know what that might be? If you fill the tub too high and then get into the water, you would cause a small flood without this feature. Pools and decorative fountains use the same principle to prevent overflow.

Thinking Critically How does placing the solid in the glass first prevent displacement?

▲ **Figure 2-16** Displacement can cause spill-over if you're not careful.

LAB ACTIVITY
Comparing Densities of Coins

Materials

Safety goggles,
triple-beam balance,
25-mL graduated
cylinder, calculator,
10 pennies, 10 nickels,
10 dimes, water,
eyedropper, plastic
cup, paper towels

▲ **STEP 3** Fill the graduated cylinder to exactly 10 mL.

▲ **Figure 2-17** The water level should be at 10 mL.

BACKGROUND

You have just learned that matter has two basic properties. They are mass, which is the amount of material in an object, and volume, the amount of space that an object takes up. Dividing the mass of an object by its volume gives the density of the object, another property of matter. We will be finding the density of various coins using the displacement method.

PURPOSE

In this activity, you will observe and predict the density of the materials that make up pennies, nickels, and dimes using the displacement method. To do this, you will use 10 of each coin so that the measurements are easy to make.

PROCEDURE

1. Copy the chart in Figure 2-18.

2. Predict whether or not the densities of the coins will be different from each other. On what do you base your prediction?

3. Using the eyedropper, put exactly 10 mL of water into the 25-mL graduated cylinder as shown in Figure 2-17.

4. Find the mass of 10 pennies on the triple-beam balance and record it in the chart.

5. Carefully lower the pennies into the graduated cylinder. The water level should go up. Measure and record the new volume of the water.

6. Subtract 10 from the new volume of water to find the volume of the coins. Record this in the chart.

▲ **STEP 4** Find the mass of 10 pennies.

▲ **STEP 8** Record the volume of water when 10 dimes are added to 10 mL of water.

7. Now find the masses of 10 nickels and 10 dimes. Record the masses in the chart.

8. Repeat steps 4–6 for the 10 nickels and 10 dimes. Record the results in your chart.

Experiment	Mass (g)	Volume of Water (mL)	New Volume of Water (mL)	Volume of Coins (mL)	Density of Coins (g/mL)
10 pennies		10			
10 nickels		10			
10 dimes		10			

▲ **Figure 2-18** Copy this chart and use it to record your observations.

CONCLUSIONS

1. **CALCULATE:** Find the density of each coin. Divide the mass of coins by the volume of coins. Complete the chart.

2. **COMPARE:** How does your prediction compare with the actual results?

3. **INFER:** Which has a greater density, 10 pennies or 10 nickels? Explain why.

4. **INFER:** Which has a greater density, 10 pennies or 10 dimes? Explain why.

5. **APPLY:** How would you find the density of a quarter? Explain your reasoning.

2-5 What is buoyancy?

Objective

Explain Archimedes' principle in terms of buoyancy and displacement.

Key Terms

buoyancy (BOI-uhn-see): tendency of an object to float in a fluid

newton: SI unit of force

Archimedes' Principle When Archimedes stepped into a bathtub, he observed the water level rising. As he sat down, he also noticed that his body seemed to feel lighter. Archimedes hypothesized that the rising of the water in the tub and his feeling of weight loss must be related. Upon further investigation, he found that the weight "lost" by an object in water is equal to the weight of the water displaced by the object. This is called Archimedes' principle.

▶ **1** STATE: What does Archimedes' principle state?

Buoyancy When an object is placed in water, it seems to weigh less than it does in air. The water exerts an upward force on the object. This upward force opposes the downward pull of gravity on the object, thus decreasing its weight. This upward force is responsible for buoyancy. **Buoyancy** is the tendency of an object to float in a fluid. Fluids are gases, such as air, or liquids, such as water.

You can observe buoyancy in action when you watch a person or a boat float on the surface of water. You can experience buoyancy yourself by standing in the shallow end of a swimming pool and lifting your leg. Your leg will seem very light. Your leg feels light because the buoyant force of the water is helping to hold up your leg.

▶ **2** DEFINE: What is buoyancy?

Buoyancy and Archimedes' Principle Archimedes' principle states that the amount of weight lost by an object in water is equal to the weight of the water that the object displaces. Buoyancy is related to displacement. The buoyant, or upward, force on an object in water is equal to the weight of the water that the object displaces. Look at Figure 2-19. The weight of the rock is shown in newtons (N). The **newton** is the SI unit of force. One kilogram equals 9.8N. If a rock weighing 4N displaces an amount of water weighing 1N, the buoyant force on the rock is 1N. The rock's weight in the water is 4N − 1N, or 3N.

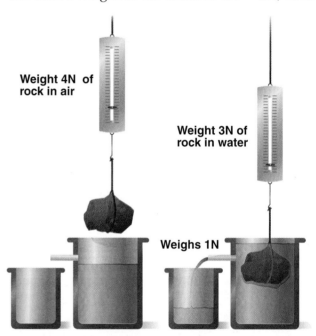

Weight 4N of rock in air

Weight 3N of rock in water

Weighs 1N

▲ **Figure 2-19** The weight lost by the rock when placed in water equals the weight of water displaced by the rock.

▶ **3** APPLY: If a buoyant force of 6 N acts on a block placed in water, what is the weight of the water that the block displaces?

Floating Buoyancy explains why an object sinks or floats. Suppose that an object displaces enough water so that the weight of the displaced water is equal to its own weight. Then, the buoyant force on the object will be equal to the object's weight. As a result, the weight of the object in water is zero. The object floats. An object sinks if its weight is greater than the buoyant force.

 RECOGNIZE: When will an object float in water?

✔ CHECKING CONCEPTS

1. Buoyancy is the _____ force exerted by a gas or a liquid.
2. The buoyant force on an object is equal to the weight of the water it _____.
3. When the buoyant force on an object is equal to or greater than its weight, the object _____.
4. Buoyancy decreases the downward pull of _____ on an object.

5. Archimedes' principle states the amount of weight lost by an object in water equals the _____ of the displaced water.

 THINKING CRITICALLY

6. **CALCULATE: a.** A metal block is 20 cm long, 10 cm high, and 5 cm wide. If submerged in water, how much water will the block displace? **b.** If the density of water is 1 g/cm^3, what will be the buoyant force on the block?
7. **EXPLAIN:** How are displacement and buoyant force related?

HEALTH AND SAFETY TIP

Always wear a life jacket if you go sailing or canoeing. If you fall into the water, the air in the jacket will decrease your overall density and help you to float, even if you cannot swim. Visit a local swimming pool. Ask the swimming instructor to describe how people are taught to float.

 Science and Technology

SUBMARINE BALLAST

Submarines are specialized ships that travel on or under the surface of water. This is possible because the buoyancy of a submarine can be changed. Submarines have special containers called ballast tanks. Ballast tanks can be filled with either air or water, helping them float or sink.

Submarines are made of steel and other heavy materials. But, when a submarine's ballast tanks are full of air, the average density of the whole ship is less than the density of water. So, the buoyant force of water makes the submarine float.

To dive, the ballast tanks are flooded with water. This added weight makes the average density of the ship greater than the density of water. The buoyant force no longer supports the ship, and it sinks. To resurface, compressed air forces water out of the tanks. This action makes the submarine lighter again.

Thinking Critically What might happen if a ballast tank were to leak?

When a submarine is on the surface, its ballast tanks are full of air. This keeps it afloat.

To dive, water is pumped into the ballast tanks, making the submarine heavier.

To rise, air forces water out of the ballast tanks, making the submarine lighter.

▲ **Figure 2-20** How ballast tanks help submarines change their buoyancy

THE Big IDEA

How has shipbuilding changed throughout history?

How do you build a boat that will float? A boat floats when the weight of the water it displaces is equal to the weight of the boat itself. The more water the boat displaces, the greater the load it can carry.

Buoyancy is the tendency for an object to float in a fluid. Humans have made buoyant watercraft for ages. One ancient design is a raft built with a low-density material, like reeds or bamboo. A raft displaces water and remains buoyant, even though water may flow all around and through the raft. The first people of Australia probably arrived there from Asia

Bamboo Rafts, Circa B.C. 38,000

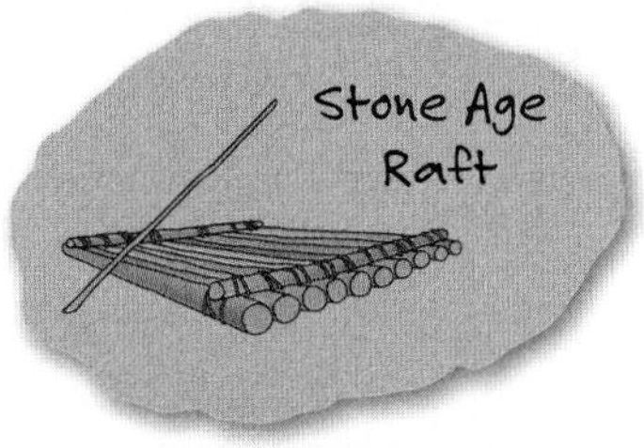

Stone Age Raft

We can only guess what the boats looked like. However, there is strong evidence that the first people of New Guinea and Australia arrived in those countries on bamboo rafts 30,000 to 40,000 years ago.

Tree Trunk Canoes, Circa B.C. 1000

Around 1000 B.C., Polynesian sailors began to travel to the remote islands of the western Pacific. Their boats were made from hollowed tree trunks and planks lashed together with coconut fibers. The outrigger design gives stability. Double outrigger sailing canoes can make long ocean voyages.

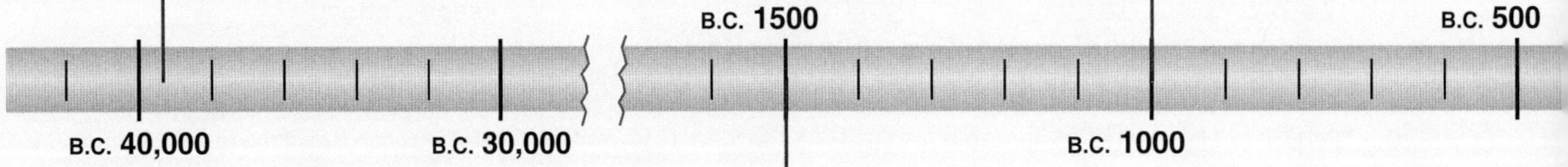

Pacific Sailing Canoe

B.C. **1500**   B.C. **500**

B.C. **40,000**   B.C. **30,000**   B.C. **1000**

Reed Rafts, B.C. 1500

Egyptian Raft

Pharaohs were buried with models of the boats that were used in Egypt in ancient times.

▲ **Figure 2-21** Shipbuilding throughout history

by floating on bamboo rafts. Ancient Egyptians used reed bundles to float on the Nile.

Another boat design is the watertight hull. A boat with a watertight hull encloses an air space that displaces water, giving buoyancy. The hull can be made of a material much more dense than water, like steel, iron, or even concrete. If the hull springs a leak, the air space in the boat fills with water and the boat begins to sink.

Look at the timeline to compare boat designs throughout history. Then, follow the directions in the Science Log to find out more about "the big idea."✦

WRITING ACTIVITY

Science Log

Plan a voyage on one of these crafts. How would you build your boat? Where would you go? What provisions would you bring? How would you navigate? Write a story about your voyage. To learn more about replicating ancient boats, start your project at www.conceptsandchallenges.com.

Oak Plank Long Ship, Circa 800 A.D.

Viking Long Ship

The Vikings sailed around Europe in ships made of oak planks. Some carried dozens of oarsmen.

Steel Supertankers, 1980 A.D.

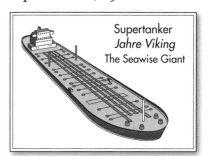

Supertanker *Jahre Viking* The Seawise Giant

One of the world's largest ships is an oil supertanker named Jahre Viking. It displaces 564,739 tons of water. It is 458 m long and 69 m wide.

500 A.D.   **1000 A.D.**   **1500 A.D.**   **2000 A.D.**

Wood and Leather Boats, 500 A.D.

The ancient "Voyage of Saint Brendan the Abbot" describes the crossing of the North Atlantic in a wood and leather boat in the sixth century. To see if this was possible, Tim Severin, a maritime historian, sailed from Ireland to Newfoundland on a replica of St. Brendan's boat.

St. Brendan's Curragh

Timber and Copper Barque, 1825 A.D.

First built as a warship, this ship changed to a survey ship in 1825. Her deck was raised and another mast was added. These changes helped in her new career as a scientific vessel. This small ship carried naturalist Charles Darwin around the world.

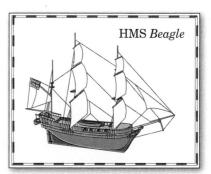

HMS *Beagle*

Chapter 2 Challenges

Chapter Summary

Lesson 2-1
- **Density** is the mass per unit volume of a substance.
- Density is measured in grams per cubic centimeter, or g/cm^3.
- Density is a basic property of all matter.
- Density can be used to identify different substances.

Lesson 2-2
- Density is equal to mass divided by volume.
- The density of a liquid can be measured in grams per milliliter or grams per cubic centimeter.
- To find the density of a solid with a regular shape, measure its mass and find its volume by multiplying its length by its width by its height.

Lesson 2-3
- **Specific gravity** is the density of a substance compared with the density of water. Specific gravity has no units.
- A **hydrometer** is a device used to measure the specific gravity of a liquid.

Lesson 2-4
- Archimedes observed that when an object is placed in water, it causes the water level to rise.
- The amount of water that an object replaces is called **displacement**.
- The volume of water that an object displaces is equal to the volume of the object.
- The volume of an irregularly shaped solid can be found by measuring how much water the object displaces.

Lesson 2-5
- Archimedes' principle states that the loss of weight of an object in water is equal to the weight of the water that the object displaces.
- **Buoyancy** is the tendency of an object to float in a fluid.
- The buoyant force on an object is equal to the weight of the water that the object displaces.
- An object floats if the weight of the water it displaces is greater than its own weight.

Key Term Challenges

buoyancy (p. 44)
density (p. 34)
displacement (p. 40)
hydrometer (p. 38)
newton (p. 44)
specific gravity (p. 38)

MATCHING Write the Key Term from above that best matches each description.

1. device used to measure specific gravity
2. tendency of an object to float in a fluid
3. density of a substance compared with the density of water
4. amount of water an object replaces
5. mass per unit volume

FILL IN Write the Key Term from above that best completes each statement.

6. To find the volume of an irregular solid, measure its _____.
7. A _____ floats high in a liquid with a high specific gravity.
8. The _____ of a substance tells the amount of mass in a certain volume.
9. A ship can float in water because of _____.
10. If the _____ of a substance is greater than 1.0, the substance is more dense than water.
11. The SI unit of force is _____.
12. If you know the density of a substance, you can easily find its _____.

Content Challenges TEST PREP

MULTIPLE CHOICE Write the letter of the term or phrase that best completes each statement.

1. Density is measured in
   a. milliliters per cubic centimeter.
   b. cubic centimeters per gram.
   c. grams per cubic centimeter.
   d. milliliters per gram.

2. Density is a basic physical property of
   a. gases.
   b. all matter.
   c. solids.
   d. liquids.

3. A hydrometer is used to measure
   a. mass.
   b. volume.
   c. length.
   d. specific gravity.

4. Archimedes discovered that objects weigh less when they
   a. have a larger volume.
   b. are placed in water.
   c. are suspended in air.
   d. are irregularly shaped.

5. The weight of the water that a floating object displaces is equal to the object's
   a. mass.
   b. weight.
   c. volume.
   d. density.

6. If the buoyant force on an object is equal to the object's weight, then the object will
   a. sink.
   b. float.
   c. become less dense.
   d. increase in mass.

7. If the buoyant force on an object is equal to the object's weight, then the weight of the object in water is
   a. 10.
   b. 100.
   c. zero.
   d. its own weight.

8. One milliliter is equal to one
   a. gram.
   b. cubic centimeter.
   c. meter.
   d. centimeter.

9. To find the density of a substance, you must measure
   a. mass and length.
   b. mass and weight.
   c. mass and volume.
   d. mass and buoyancy.

10. If a rock displaces 50 mL, the volume of the rock is
    a. 50 cm.
    b. 50 g/cm^3.
    c. 5 mL.
    d. 50 cm^3.

TRUE/FALSE Write *true* if the statement is true. If the statement is false, change the underlined term to make the statement true.

11. Specific gravity compares the density of a substance to the <u>weight</u> of water.

12. Units of <u>density</u> include units of mass and volume.

13. <u>Displacement</u> is a force exerted upward by a gas or a liquid.

14. When an object is placed in water, it will lose all or some of its <u>mass</u>.

15. The buoyant force on an object is equal to the <u>volume</u> of the water it displaces.

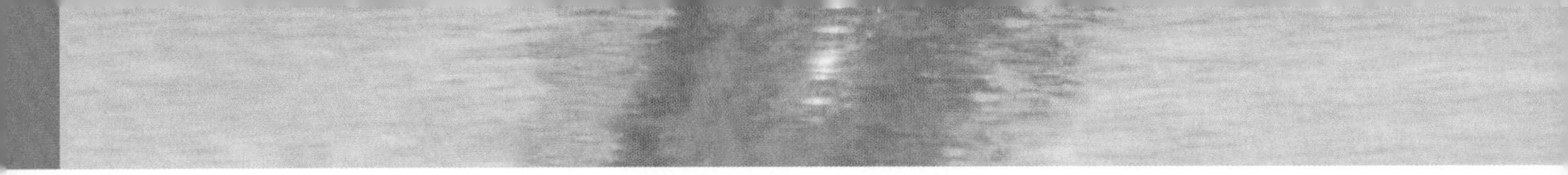

Concept Challenges

WRITTEN RESPONSE Answer each of the following questions in complete sentences.

1. **EXPLAIN:** Why is 1 cm³ of wood lighter than 1 cm³ of iron?

2. **ANALYZE:** Suppose two objects look alike, but one is made of marble and the other is made of plastic. How could you use specific gravity to identify the objects?

3. **EXPLAIN:** Why is it possible to measure the volume of a solid in milliliters?

4. **RELATE:** What is the relationship between the density of a substance and its specific gravity?

5. **RELATE:** What is the relationship between the buoyant force on an object and the amount of water that the object displaces?

6. **INFER:** What do you know about the density of an object that floats in water?

INTERPRETING A TABLE Use Figure 2-22 to answer the following questions.

7. **NAME:** What is the specific gravity of gold?

8. **INTERPRET:** Which substance has a higher specific gravity, diamond or glycerine?

9. **NAME:** What are two substances that will float in water?

10. **PREDICT:** What will happen if water and corn syrup are mixed together?

11. **ANALYZE:** Which will take up a greater volume, a kilogram of lead or a kilogram of rubber?

12. **ANALYZE:** Will a hydrometer float higher in glycerine or in gasoline? Explain.

SPECIFIC GRAVITIES	
Substance	**Specific Gravity**
Aluminum	2.7
Corn syrup	1.38
Diamond	3.5
Gasoline	0.7
Glycerine	1.26
Gold	19.3
Ice	0.92
Marble	2.7
Rubber	1.34
Water	1.00

▲ Figure 2-22

Chapter 3 Elements and Atoms

▲ **Figure 3-1** Bars of gold

Gold is one of the few things that can be found on Earth in pure form. If you could cut a bar of gold into smaller pieces, you would find that the smallest piece that could be identified as gold is one atom of gold. This atom is made up of even smaller parts. These very tiny parts are not gold. They can be found in all forms of matter. However, it is difficult to see them. Special tools are needed in order to study these small pieces of matter.

▶Why is it difficult to study small pieces of matter?

Contents

3-1 What are elements?

INVESTIGATE

Observing Matter
HANDS-ON ACTIVITY

1. Copy the chart onto a sheet of paper. Your teacher will give you different models of matter. Examine each model. Notice how each one is made up of smaller, different-colored pieces.

2. Fill in the chart. The first line has been completed for you.

THINK ABOUT IT: How many models of matter are there? How many smaller pieces are there in each type of matter?

Observing Matter	
Model of Matter	What is it made of?
A	●●
B	
C	
D	

▲ **Figure 3-2** Model A is made up of two red circles.

Objective
Identify elements as substances that cannot be chemically broken down into simpler substances.

Key Term
element (EHL-uh-muhnt): substance that cannot be chemically broken down into simpler substances

Elements Most of the objects around you are made up of combinations of different kinds of matter. For example, the concrete in a sidewalk is made up of different types of matter—gravel, sand, cement, and water. However, even gravel, sand, cement, and water are made from other types of matter. But these types of matter, called elements, are different. **Elements** are substances that cannot be chemically broken down into simpler substances. All of the matter that you can observe on Earth is made up of elements or combinations of elements.

 DEFINE: What is an element?

The Known Elements There are more than 100 known elements. Most of the first ninety-two elements are found in nature. The rest of the elements have been made by scientists under special laboratory conditions.

Most elements are solids at room temperature. Some examples that you may be familiar with are iron, zinc, lead, silver, gold, calcium, sodium, nickel, and copper.

A few elements, such as mercury and bromine, are liquids at room temperature. Other elements, such as oxygen, hydrogen, helium, and neon, are gases at room temperature.

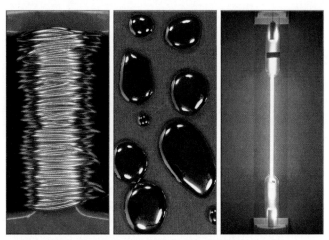

▲ **Figure 3-3** At room temperature, copper (left) is a solid, mercury (center) is a liquid, and neon (right) is a gas.

 IDENTIFY: How many elements are found in nature?

Elements and Matter All matter is made up of elements. Some types of matter are made up of only one element. An iron nail may contain only the element iron. Aluminum foil may be made up of only the element aluminum. Pure gold and pure silver are also made up of only one element.

There are some types of matter that are made up of more than one element. Water is made up of hydrogen and oxygen. Table salt is made up of sodium and chlorine.

In a laboratory, a chemist can break down this kind of matter. For example, sugar can be broken down into the elements that make it up—carbon, hydrogen, and oxygen. These elements cannot be chemically broken down into simpler substances.

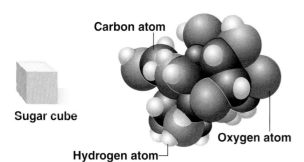

▲ Figure 3-4 Sugar can be broken down into the elements that make it up.

▶ NAME: What three elements make up sugar?

✓ CHECKING CONCEPTS

1. An _____ is a substance that cannot be chemically broken down into simpler substances.

2. Mercury is a _____ at room temperature.

3. There are more than _____ known elements.

4. Most of the known elements are _____ at room temperature.

5. An example of a substance made up of more than one element is _____.

💡 THINKING CRITICALLY

6. COMPARE: Mercury and oxygen are elements. Explain one way in which they differ from each other.

7. CLASSIFY: Which of the following substances are elements?
   a. Gold
   c. Mercury
   b. Hydrogen
   d. Sugar

HEALTH AND SAFETY TIP

Many elements are dangerous to handle. The elements mercury and chlorine are poisonous. Sodium and potassium are explosive when exposed to water. Review the rules for chemical safety in the Handbook on page 14. Make a poster illustrating some chemical safety rules.

People in Science

MARIE CURIE (1867–1934)

Marie Sklodowska Curie was a Polish chemist. She worked and taught in Paris at the School of Physics and Chemistry and at the Sorbonne, the University of Paris. While teaching in Paris, she met the French scientist Pierre Curie, who became her husband.

Marie and Pierre Curie worked together. They became interested in radioactive (ray-dee-oh-AK-tihv) elements. Radioactive elements give off a form of energy known as radiation (ray-dee-AY-shuhn). Two years after radioactivity was first discovered in the element uranium, the Curies discovered the radioactive elements polonium and radium. In 1903, the Curies were awarded a Nobel Prize in physics.

▲ Figure 3-5 Marie Curie studied radioactive elements.

After the death of her husband in 1906, Marie Curie continued to study radioactive elements. In 1911, she was awarded a Nobel Prize in chemistry. Marie Curie is the only person ever to receive two Nobel Prizes in science.

Thinking Critically Why do you think Marie Curie was an important scientist?

3-2 What are atoms?

Objectives

Identify an atom as the smallest part of an element that can be identified as that element. List the main parts of Dalton's atomic theory.

Key Term

atom: smallest part of an element that can be identified as that element

Atoms

The element silicon cannot be broken down into a simpler type of matter. But what would happen if you took a piece of silicon and cut it into smaller and smaller pieces? There would be a piece of silicon so small that it could not be further divided. This smallest piece of the element silicon is called an atom. An **atom** is the smallest part of an element that can be identified as that element.

▶ **INFER:** What would happen if you cut a piece of an element into smaller and smaller pieces?

Democritus

The first person to suggest the idea of atoms was the Greek philosopher Democritus (dih-MAHK-ruh-tuhs). More than 2,400 years ago, Democritus asked whether it is possible to divide a sample of matter forever into smaller and smaller pieces. After much observation, he came to the conclusion that it is not possible to divide matter forever. At some point, a smallest piece of matter would be reached. Democritus named this smallest piece of matter an atom. The word *atom* comes from a Greek word that means "cannot be divided."

Democritus and his students did not know what atoms looked liked. They did not know what scientists today know about atoms. However, they hypothesized that atoms were small, hard particles that were all made out of the same material but were of different shapes and sizes. They also thought that atoms were infinite in number, that they were always moving, and that they could be joined together.

▶ **STATE:** What does the word *atom* mean?

Dalton's Atomic Theory

In the early 1800s, an English chemist named John Dalton performed some experiments. He investigated properties of gases. His observations led him to believe that gases are made of individual particles. These individual particles are very similar to the idea of the atom proposed by Democritus. The results of his experiments and other observations about matter led Dalton to state an atomic theory of matter. The main parts of Dalton's atomic theory of matter are as follows:

- All elements are composed of atoms. Atoms cannot be divided or destroyed.

- Atoms of the same element are exactly alike.

- Atoms of different elements are different from each other.

- The atoms of two or more elements can join together to form types of matter called compounds.

Like Democritus, Dalton had some ideas about atoms that scientists no longer agree with. However, Dalton's atomic theory was the beginning of the modern theory of atoms.

▲ **Figure 3-6** John Dalton

▶ **LIST:** What are the main parts of Dalton's atomic theory of matter?

Images of Atoms Atoms are extremely small. As small as they are, a special tool, called a scanning tunneling microscope (STM), can capture images of them. Figure 3-7 shows an image captured by an STM.

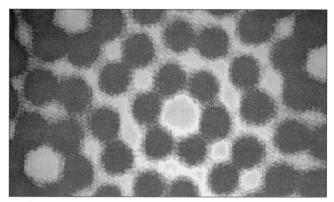

▲ **Figure 3-7** An image of silicon atoms produced by an STM

 NAME: What is an STM?

☑ CHECKING CONCEPTS

1. What is an atom?
2. Who was the first person to use the word *atom?*

3. Whose investigation on properties of gases led him to propose an atomic theory of matter?
4. What is the name of the tool that can capture images of an atom?

💡 THINKING CRITICALLY

5. **COMPARE:** How are the ideas of Democritus and Dalton similar? How are they different?
6. **INFER:** How can an STM help prove Dalton's theory?

Web InfoSearch

Scanning Tunneling Microscopes STMs can take images of atoms.

SEARCH: Use the Internet to find out about the inventors of this type of microscope. Start your search at www.conceptsandchallenges.com. Some key search words are **Heinrich Rohrer** and **Gerd Karl Binnig**.

 Science and Technology

PARTICLE ACCELERATORS

A particle accelerator is a device used to increase the energy of electrically charged particles. At very high speeds, these charged particles smash into atoms and break them apart. Then, scientists can study the pieces that are left after the collision.

▲ **Figure 3-8** In Batavia, Illinois, a particle accelerator lies under the circular outline.

Scientists use particle accelerators to study the forces that hold matter together. The machines speed up particles and race them around and around giant, usually circular, tracks. Many accelerators have one group of particles moving in one direction and another group moving in the other direction. When the particles are traveling fast enough, they are made to crash into each other. From their work with accelerators, scientists have been able to learn more about the parts that atoms are made of.

Particle accelerators are among the largest instruments ever built. In Batavia, Illinois, a particle accelerator is built around a 6.4-km circular track. A particle accelerator in Switzerland is build in a circular underground tunnel that is 27 km wide.

Thinking Critically Why do you think particle accelerators are so large?

3-3 What are the parts of an atom?

Objective
Identify the three basic parts of an atom.

Key Terms
nucleus: center, or core, of an atom
proton: particle that has a positive charge
neutron: particle that has no charge
electron: particle that has a negative charge

Structure of an Atom According to the modern atomic theory, an atom has a center, or core, called the **nucleus**. In the nucleus are protons and neutrons. A **proton** is a particle that has a positive charge (+). A **neutron** is a particle that does not have any charge. Surrounding the nucleus is a cloud of very tiny particles called electrons. An **electron** is a particle that has a negative charge (–). The negative charge on an electron is exactly equal to the positive charge on a proton.

1 STATE: Where is the nucleus found?

Thomson's Model The first scientist to suggest that an atom contains smaller particles was J. J. Thomson of England. In 1897, Thomson passed an electric current through a gas. He found that the gas gave off rays made up of negatively charged particles. Today, these particles are known as electrons. Because atoms are neutral, Thomson reasoned that there must also be positively charged particles inside an atom. Thomson hypothesized that an atom was made up of a positively charged material with negatively charged particles scattered evenly throughout.

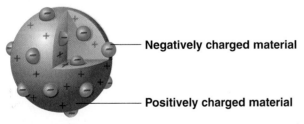

Negatively charged material

Positively charged material

▲ Figure 3-9 Thomson's model of an atom

2 IDENTIFY: What type of particle did Thomson discover in an atom?

Rutherford's Model
In 1911, a British scientist named Ernest Rutherford performed an experiment to test Thomson's atomic model. Rutherford discovered that an atom is mostly empty space. He concluded that the positively charged particles are contained in a small central core

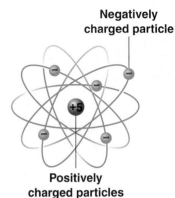

Negatively charged particle

Positively charged particles

▲ Figure 3-10 Rutherford's model of an atom

called the nucleus. He also concluded that the negatively charged particles were attracted to the positively charged particles found in the nucleus. This attraction holds the negatively charged particles in the atom.

3 DESCRIBE: What did Rutherford discover about an atom?

Bohr's Model
Rutherford's model of the atom was useful but it did not explain the arrangement of electrons. In 1913, Danish scientist Niels Bohr proposed that the electrons in an atom are found in

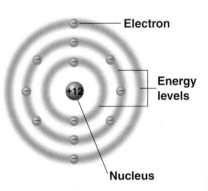

Electron

Energy levels

Nucleus

▲ Figure 3-11 Bohr's model of an atom

different energy levels. Each energy level is at a certain distance from the nucleus. Electrons in different energy levels move around the nucleus in different orbits, much as the planets move in orbits around the Sun. Bohr's model explains simple atoms such as oxygen well, but it does not explain more complex atoms.

4 LOCATE: Where did Bohr say that electrons are found in an atom?

Modern Model The modern atomic model is based on the works of Thomson, Rutherford, Bohr, and other scientists who have studied the nature of atoms. According to the modern model, the location of the electrons in an atom cannot be known. Therefore, the modern model of the atom does not show any paths that electrons could be found in. Instead, energy levels are used to predict the place where an electron is most likely to be found outside of the nucleus. This area is called the electron cloud. The modern model also identifies the nucleus as containing protons and neutrons.

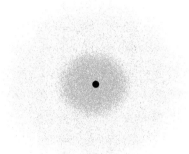

◄ **Figure 3-12** Modern model of an atom

 EXPLAIN: What is the electron cloud?

 CHECKING CONCEPTS

1. What are electrons?
2. Where are protons found in an atom?
3. What are the particles in an atom that do not have any charge called?
4. Who first suggested that atoms are made up of smaller particles?
5. Who discovered that an atom is mostly empty space?
6. Who proposed the idea that electrons are found in different energy levels around the nucleus?

 THINKING CRITICALLY

7. **CONTRAST:** How did Rutherford's model of the atom differ from Thomson's model?
8. **EXPLAIN:** According to the modern atomic model, where are protons, neutrons, and electrons found?

How Do They Know That?

QUARKS AND LEPTONS

In recent years, scientists have discovered that protons and neutrons are made up of even smaller particles. Based on experiments using particle accelerators, scientists have identified two groups of subatomic particles. All matter is made up of these particles. These groups of particles are known as quarks and leptons. The word *quark* was first used as the name of a subatomic particle by American physicist Murray Gell-Mann. The word *lepton* comes from a Greek word that means "small" or "thin."

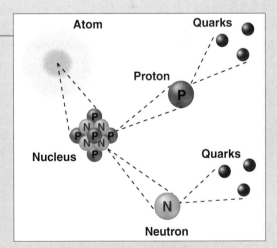

▲ **Figure 3-13** Protons and neutrons are made up of quarks.

Quarks make up protons, neutrons, and other particles found in the nucleus of an atom. There are six types of quarks and six types of leptons. Electrons are a type of lepton. Electrons are not believed to be made up of smaller particles. The basic particles in an atom are made up of combinations of two or three different quarks or one lepton.

Thinking Critically What is the relationship between an electron and a lepton?

3-4 What is an atomic number?

Objective

Explain what is meant by the atomic number of an element.

Key Term

atomic number: number of protons in the nucleus of an atom

Elements and Atomic Number The atoms of different elements have different numbers of protons. You have learned that protons are particles that have a positive charge (+) and are found within the nucleus of an atom. The number of protons found in the nucleus of an atom is called the **atomic number**. Each element has a different atomic number because the atoms of each element have a different number of protons in their nuclei.

The element with the smallest atomic number is hydrogen. Hydrogen has an atomic number of 1. This means that an atom of hydrogen has only one proton in its nucleus. Oxygen has an atomic number of 8 because there are 8 protons in the nucleus of an atom of oxygen. Gold has an atomic number of 79. There are 79 protons in an atom of gold. Figure 3-15 lists the atomic numbers of some common elements. Figure 3-14 shows the nuclei of the elements helium, beryllium, and neon. You can see that the number of protons in the nuclei of each element is the same as the atomic number of each element.

ATOMIC NUMBERS OF SOME ELEMENTS	
Element	**Atomic number**
Hydrogen	1
Helium	2
Carbon	6
Nitrogen	7
Oxygen	8
Sodium	11
Aluminum	13
Sulfur	16
Chlorine	17
Calcium	20
Iron	26
Copper	29
Silver	47
Gold	79
Lead	82

▲ Figure 3-15

 DEFINE: What is an atomic number?

Importance of Atomic Number Your fingerprint is very important because it identifies you. No other person can have the same fingerprint as yours. The atomic number of an element is very important because it identifies that element. No two elements have the same atomic number. In fact, the number of protons in the nucleus of an atom tells you what that element is.

2 EXPLAIN: Why is the atomic number of an element important?

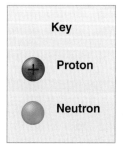

Key

Proton

Neutron

Helium
Atomic number = 2

Beryllium
Atomic number = 4

Neon
Atomic number = 10

▲ **Figure 3-14** The nuclei of helium, beryllium, and neon

Atomic Number and Electrons If you know the atomic number of an element, you also know the number of electrons in an atom of that element. They are both the same number. They are the same because an atom has neither a positive nor a negative charge. It is neutral. In order for an atom to be neutral, the positive charges of the protons and the negative charges of the electrons must cancel each other out. So the number of electrons must be the same as the number of protons.

 CALCULATE: How many electrons are there in an atom of an element with an atomic number of 14?

✔ CHECKING CONCEPTS

1. The atomic number is the number of _____ in the nucleus of an atom.
2. Every _____ has its own atomic number.
3. The element with the smallest atomic number is _____.

4. No two elements have the same _____.
5. The number of protons in an atom is equal to the number of _____ in the atom.

💡 THINKING CRITICALLY

6. **ANALYZE:** If an atom has an atomic number of 12, how many electrons does the atom have?
7. **EXPLAIN:** How can knowing the atomic number of an atom help you to identify the element?

INTERPRETING VISUALS

Use Figure 3-15 to answer the following questions.

8. **IDENTIFY:** What is the atomic number of calcium?
9. **IDENTIFY:** How many protons are there in an atom of copper?
10. **NAME:** What element has an atomic number of 13?
11. **IDENTIFY:** How many electrons are there in an atom of aluminum?

 People in Science
CHIEN-SHIUNG WU (1912–1997)

▲ **Figure 3-16** Chien-Shiung Wu studied beta decay.

Chien-Shiung Wu was born in Liu Ho, China. She was a theoretical physicist. Chien-Shiung Wu came to America in 1936 to study for a doctorate in physics. She received her Ph.D. from the University of California at Berkeley. During World War II, she taught physics at Smith College and at Princeton University. After the war, she went to Columbia University to do research in nuclear physics. She became a professor of physics at Columbia in 1957.

Chien-Shiung Wu's area of specialization was beta decay. In beta decay, the nucleus of an atom gives off electrons. This causes the atom to change into another element. Chien-Shiung Wu made many important contributions to scientists' present knowledge of the atom. Her experiments on beta decay confirmed a theory proposed by two other scientists. These scientists, Tsung Dao Lee and Chen Ning Yang, later won a Nobel Prize for their theory. Chien-Shiung Wu was the first woman to receive the Comstock Prize from the National Academy of Sciences.

Thinking Critically How did Chien-Shiung Wu's work contribute to the work of other scientists?

3-5 What is an atomic mass?

INVESTIGATE

Making a Model of a Nucleus
HANDS-ON ACTIVITY

1. Obtain colored disks, plastic wrap, and wire-ties from your teacher. Place two red disks and two blue disks in the center of a small piece of plastic wrap. Use a wire-tie to wrap the plastic around the disks.

2. Wrap and tie six red disks and six blue disks using another piece of plastic wrap.

3. Count the total number of disks inside each bag.

STEP 1

THINK ABOUT IT: If each "bundle" represents the nucleus of an atom, what does each colored disk represent? What does the total number of disks inside each bag represent?

Objective

Explain how to find the atomic mass and the mass number of an atom.

Key Terms

atomic mass: total mass of the protons and neutrons in an atom, measured in atomic mass units (amu)

mass number: number of protons and neutrons in the nucleus of an atom

Atomic Mass Unit Imagine trying to measure the mass of something so small that you cannot see it. Well, scientists do just that when they measure the mass of an atom. The mass of an atom is very small. It is not easy to measure the mass of an atom in grams. So, in order to measure the mass of an atom, scientists have developed a special unit. This unit is called the atomic mass unit, or amu.

One amu is equal to the mass of one proton. Neutrons and protons have almost the same mass. Therefore, one amu is also equal to the mass of one neutron. The mass of an electron is equal to 1/1,836 amu. Because electrons are so small, only the masses of protons and neutrons are used to find the mass of an atom.

 INFER: What is the mass, in amu, of an atom with one proton and two neutrons?

Atomic Mass The total mass of the protons and neutrons in an atom is called the **atomic mass**. Atomic mass is measured in atomic mass units (amu). Because the atoms of an element can have different numbers of neutrons, scientists often give the average atomic mass for an element.

 DEFINE: What is an atomic mass?

Mass Number The total number of protons and neutrons in an atom is called the **mass number**. You can find the mass number for any element. The mass number can be found by rounding the average atomic mass to the nearest whole number. For example, the average atomic mass of lithium is 6.941 amu. The mass number of lithium is 7 (6.941 rounds to 7).

AVERAGE ATOMIC MASS AND MASS NUMBER		
Element	**Average atomic mass**	**Mass number**
Hydrogen	1.008	1
Helium	4.003	4
Carbon	12.011	12
Oxygen	15.999	16

▲ **Figure 3-17** To find the mass number, round the average atomic mass to the nearest whole number.

 DEFINE: What is mass number?

Finding Neutrons If you know the atomic number and the mass number of an element, then you can find the number of neutrons in an atom of the most common form of that element. You can use the following formula:

$$\text{mass number} - \text{atomic number} = \text{number of neutrons}$$

Look at Figure 3-18 to find the number of neutrons in an atom of lithium.

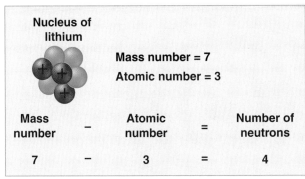

Nucleus of lithium

Mass number = 7
Atomic number = 3

Mass number	–	Atomic number	=	Number of neutrons
7	–	3	=	4

▲ **Figure 3-18** You can find the number of neutrons in an atom of the most common form of lithium.

 4 ANALYZE: How many neutrons are in the nucleus of an atom of carbon?

✓ CHECKING CONCEPTS

1. The mass of a neutron is the same as the mass of a _____.
2. Because they are so small, _____ are not counted when measuring the mass of an atom.
3. The _____ is the unit used by scientists to measure the mass of an atom.
4. The mass number tells the total number of _____ and neutrons in the nucleus of an atom.

THINKING CRITICALLY

5. **ANALYZE:** Explain why the mass number of an element can never be less than the atomic number of that element.
6. **INFER:** Why is the mass of an electron not added to the atomic mass of an atom?

BUILDING MATH SKILLS

Calculating The atomic number of element x is 30 and the mass number is 65. Find the number of protons, neutrons, and electrons in an atom of element x.

People in Science

DMITRI MENDELEEV (1834–1907)

Dmitri Mendeleev (men-duh-LAY-uhf) was a Russian chemist. He was a professor of chemistry at St. Petersburg University in Russia. He is best known for developing the first table of elements organized according to properties.

Mendeleev wrote a book called *Principles of Chemistry.* For this book, Mendeleev collected thousands of facts about the 63 elements that were known at that time. He tried to find a way to organize this information. He thought that a certain pattern, or order, of the elements must exist.

▲ **Figure 3-19** Dmitri Mendeleev

Mendeleev decided to test his hypothesis. He wrote the name of each element and the properties of that element on a card. Then, he tried different arrangements of the cards for the 63 elements. When he arranged the cards in order of increasing atomic mass, the elements fell into groups with similar properties.

Thinking Critically Why do you think it was important to Mendeleev to organize his information into a table?

3-6 How are electrons arranged in an atom?

Objective
Describe how the electrons in an atom are arranged in energy levels.

Key Term
energy level: place in an electron cloud where an electron is most likely to be found

The Electron Cloud For many years, scientists thought that electrons moved around the nucleus of an atom in much the same way as the planets orbit the Sun. Scientists now know that it is not possible to predict the exact path of an electron. You have learned that the area in an atom where electrons are likely to be found is called the electron cloud. Scientists use the word *cloud* because they know that they cannot predict the exact location of electrons nor the speed at which electrons move at any given time.

▶ **DESCRIBE:** What is an electron cloud?

Energy Levels According to the modern atomic theory, electrons are arranged in energy levels around the nucleus of an atom. An **energy level** is the place in the electron cloud where an electron is most likely to be found. Each energy level is a different distance from the nucleus. The lowest, or first, energy level is closest to the nucleus. Electrons with more energy are found in energy levels farther away from the nucleus.

Each energy level can hold only a certain number of electrons. The first energy level can hold only two electrons. The second energy level can hold up to eight electrons. The third energy level can hold up to 18 electrons. The fourth energy level can hold up to 32 electrons. For the elements with atomic numbers between 1 and 20, the electrons in an atom of an element fill up the energy levels in order, beginning with the lowest.

An atom of helium has two electrons. These two electrons fill the first energy level. An atom of lithium has three electrons. Two of these electrons fill the first energy level. The third electron occupies the second energy level. An atom of chlorine has 17 electrons. Two electrons fill the first energy level, eight electrons fill the second level, and seven electrons occupy the third level.

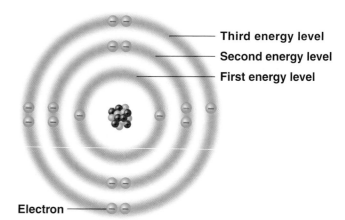

Third energy level
Second energy level
First energy level

Electron

▲ **Figure 3-20** An atom of chlorine has three energy levels. The first two energy levels are completely filled. Seven electrons occupy the third energy level.

▶ **PREDICT:** Where would you expect to find the six electrons in an atom of carbon?

Changing Energy Levels Adding energy to an atom or removing energy from an atom can cause the electrons in the atom to move from one energy level to another. If an electron gains enough energy, it jumps to a higher energy level. When this happens, the atom is in an "excited" state.

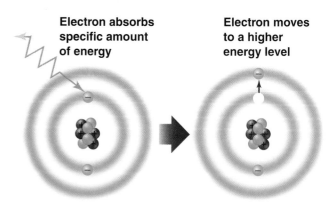

Electron absorbs specific amount of energy

Electron moves to a higher energy level

▲ **Figure 3-21** In an "excited" state, an electron jumps to a higher energy level.

If an electron in an excited atom loses enough energy, it drops back to a lower energy level. As it drops back, the electron gives off energy, often in the form of light.

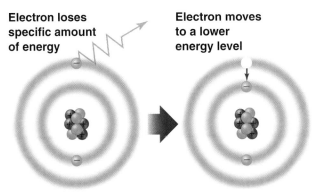

Electron loses specific amount of energy

Electron moves to a lower energy level

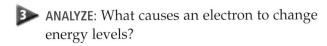

▲ **Figure 3-22** When an electron in an excited state loses energy, it drops to a lower energy level.

 ANALYZE: What causes an electron to change energy levels?

✓ CHECKING CONCEPTS

1. An energy level is the place in the electron cloud where an _____ is most likely to be found in an atom.

2. The _____ energy level is located closest to the nucleus of an atom.

3. The second energy level can hold up to _____ electrons.

4. An electron will drop to a lower energy level when it _____ energy.

💡 THINKING CRITICALLY

5. **ANALYZE:** The atoms of a certain element have the first and second energy levels completely filled with electrons. What is the atomic number of this element? Explain how you know this.

Hands-On Activity

MAKING ELECTRON DOT DIAGRAMS

You will need element symbol cards, a periodic table, and a felt-tip marker.

1. An electron dot diagram is a simple way to show how the electrons in the outermost energy level of an atom are arranged. Look at the electron dot diagrams for the elements carbon, atomic number 6, and nitrogen, atomic number 7 in Figure 3-23.

2. Obtain three element symbol cards from your teacher. Notice how the element on each card has a symbol along with its atomic number.

3. Use the diagrams for carbon and nitrogen to help you make electron dot diagrams of each of your elements.

▲ **Figure 3-23**
Electron dot diagrams for carbon and nitrogen

Practicing Your Skills

4. **EXPLAIN:** Why do you need to know the atomic number of an element to complete an electron dot diagram?

5. **OBSERVE:** What pattern do you notice in the way the electron dots are arranged around the symbol?

3-7 What is the periodic table?

Shortened Names For many years, scientists had to spell out the names of all the known elements. However, in the early 1800s, a Swedish scientist named Jons Jakob Berzelius (buhr-ZEE-lee-uhs) created a new system of representing elements. This system uses letters called chemical symbols. **Chemical symbols** are a shortened way of writing the names of elements.

▶ **DEFINE:** What is a chemical symbol?

Chemical Symbols Chemical symbols are created from the name of each element. There are usually one or two letters in a chemical symbol. The first letter of a chemical symbol is always capitalized. If there is a second letter, it is written using the lowercase. For example, Ne is the chemical symbol for neon. Some chemical symbols come from the Latin name for the element. The Latin name for lead is *plumbum*. The chemical symbol is Pb. Some elements have three letters in their chemical symbols. These chemical symbols are temporary until scientists come to an agreement on their permanent names.

▶ **EXPLAIN:** How are chemical symbols written?

Arranging Elements By the 1800s, scientists had discovered many elements. They began to search for ways to organize these elements. In 1869, a Russian chemist named Dmitri Mendeleev listed the elements in order of increasing atomic mass.

Mendeleev noticed that elements with similar properties occurred periodically. The word **periodic** means "to repeat in a certain pattern." Based on the pattern he observed, Mendeleev arranged the elements in rows in a chart. Elements with similar properties were in the same column of his chart, one under the other. Mendeleev's chart was the first periodic table of elements. Figure 3-24 shows what Mendeleev's periodic table looked like.

				Ti = 50	Zr = 90	? = 180
				V = 51	Nb = 94	Ta = 18
				Cr = 52	Mo = 96	W = 18
				Mn = 55	Rh = 104, 4	Pt = 19
				Fe = 56	Rn = 104, 4	Ir = 19
				Ni = Co = 59	Pd = 106, 6	Os = 1
H = 1				Cu = 63, 4	Ag = 108	Hg = 2
	Be = 9,4	Mg = 24	Zn = 65, 2	Cd = 112	Au = 1
	B = 11	Al = 27, 4	? = 68	Ur = 116	Bi = 21
	C = 12	Si = 28	? = 70	Sn = 118	Ti = 20
	N = 14	P = 31	As = 75	Sb = 122	Pb = 2
	O = 16	S = 32	Se = 79, 4	Te = 128?	
	F = 19	Cl = 35, 5	Br = 80	J = 127	
Li = 7	Na = 23	K = 39	Rb = 85, 4	Cs = 133	
		Ca = 40	Sr = 87, 6	Ba = 137	
		? = 45	Ce = 92		
		?Er = 56	La = 94		
		?Yt = 60	Di = 95		
		?In = 75, 6	Th = 118?		

▲ **Figure 3-24** Mendeleev's periodic table

▶ **DESCRIBE:** How were elements arranged in Mendeleev's periodic table?

The Modern Periodic Table Mendeleev's periodic table was useful, but it had some problems. Some elements did not have properties similar to the other elements in the same column. The discovery of atomic numbers, which occurred about 50 years after Mendeleev's table was developed, led to a new table. By arranging the elements in order of increasing atomic number instead of increasing atomic mass, all the elements in the same column had similar properties. This new arrangement is known as the modern periodic table of elements.

▶ **COMPARE:** How is the modern periodic table different from Mendeleev's periodic table?

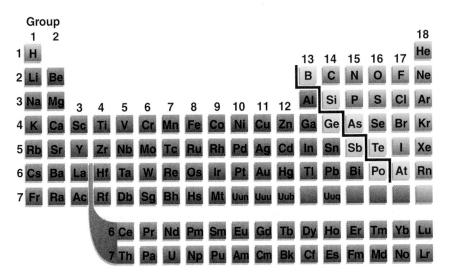

Group

◀ **Figure 3-25** A simple version of the modern Periodic Table of Elements

Groups and Periods Look at the periodic table in Figure 3-25. Notice that there are 18 columns. These columns are called **groups**, or families. Elements that are in the same group have similar physical and chemical properties. For example, lithium (Li), sodium (Na), and potassium (K) are all solids that react explosively with water. Elements in the same group also have the same number of electrons in their outermost energy levels.

The table also has seven rows. Each row is called a **period**. You can see that Period 1 has only two elements, hydrogen and helium. The elements in a period do not have similar properties. In fact, the properties of each element in a period change greatly as you move from left to right. However, there is a pattern in a period. Part of the pattern is that each period starts with an element that is a solid and ends with an element that is a gas. The first period is the only exception. Elements in the same period also have the same number of energy levels.

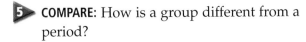 **COMPARE:** How is a group different from a period?

✔ CHECKING CONCEPTS

1. How is the first letter of a chemical symbol written?
2. How are the elements arranged in the modern periodic table?
3. What are the horizontal rows of the periodic table called?
4. How are elements in the same group similar?
5. Which scientist developed the first periodic table?

💡 THINKING CRITICALLY

6. **INFER:** Why would a scientist use Berzelius's system of representing elements?
7. **HYPOTHESIZE:** The symbol for carbon is C. The symbol for cobalt is Co. Why do you think a second letter was added to the chemical symbol of some elements? Why is the second letter written in the lowercase?

INTERPRETING VISUALS

Use Figure 3-25 to answer the following questions.

8. **IDENTIFY:** The first element in Group 17 is fluorine. What is its chemical symbol?
9. **INFER:** What group do boron (B) and thallium (Tl) belong to?
10. **NAME:** Name at least one element in Period 2.
11. **EXPLAIN:** Do you think calcium (Ca) and magnesium (Mg) have similar properties? Explain.
12. **IDENTIFY:** What group do copper (Cu) and gold (Au) belong to?
13. **IDENTIFY:** What period does iron (Fe) belong to?

BUILDING SOCIAL STUDIES SKILLS

Analyzing A few of the elements in the periodic table are named after countries, states, and planets. Use library resources, encyclopedias, or the Internet to find three of these elements. List their names and the name of the country, state, or planet for which they are named.

Integrating Physical, Earth, and Life Science

THE Big IDEA

What is the Periodic Table of Elements?

A great deal of information about the atoms that make up elements is presented in a chart called the Periodic Table of Elements. Every known element, including synthetic elements (elements made in a laboratory) is listed in the table. Information about each element, such as its name, chemical symbol, atomic number, and average atomic mass, is listed. Each element is arranged in the table in order of increasing atomic number.

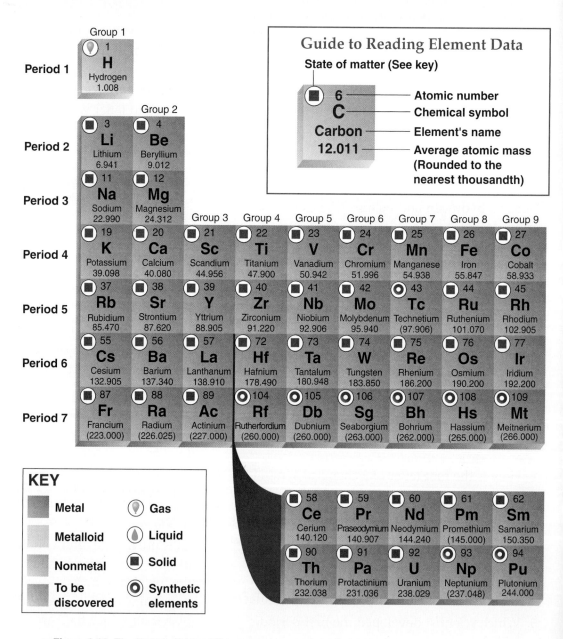

▲ **Figure 3-26** The Periodic Table of Elements

The elements that are arranged in vertical columns, called groups, have similar properties. The elements that are arranged in horizontal rows, called periods, have the same number of energy levels in each of their atoms. If more elements are discovered, they, too, will be listed in the table. The periodic table can also be used to help explain how elements combine to form every kind of matter in the universe. Elements are studied in all three major fields of science.

Look at the periodic table on these two pages. Then, follow the directions in the Science Log to find out more about "the big idea."✦

WRITING ACTIVITY

science Log

Look at the periodic table. Which elements are you familiar with? In your science log, research and write about the kinds of elements that are in the objects that you use every day. Start your search at www.conceptsandchallenges.com.

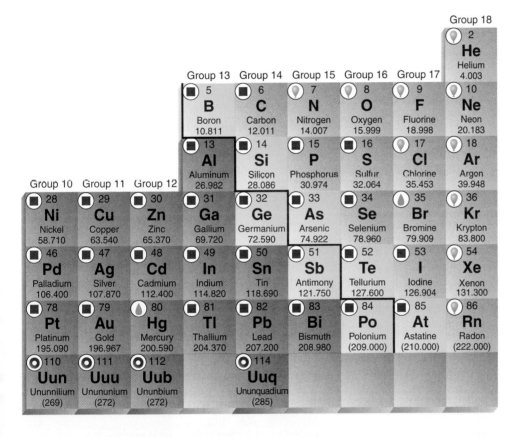

Atomic masses in parentheses are of the most common form of the atom.

3-8 What are metals and nonmetals?

Objective
Identify the properties of metals and nonmetals.

Key Terms

metal: element that has the property of shiny luster, ductility, and malleability

luster (LUS-tuhr)**:** the way a material reflects light

malleable (MAL-ee-uh-buhl)**:** able to be hammered into different shapes

ductile (DUK-tuhl)**:** able to be drawn into thin wires

nonmetal: element that lacks most of the properties of a metal

Metals and Nonmetals If you look at the periodic table, you will see a dark zigzag line running from the top of Group 13 to the bottom of Group 16. This line separates two different types of elements. The elements to the left of the line, with the exception of hydrogen, are metals. The elements to the right of the line are nonmetals.

1 NAME: What are two different types of elements?

Properties of Metals **Metals** are elements that have the properties of shiny luster, ductility, and malleability. All metals, except mercury, are solids at room temperature. Mercury is a liquid. The properties of metals are as follows:

- Some metals are shiny. A gold ring is shiny. The way a material reflects light is called its **luster**.

- Most metals are **malleable**. They can be hammered into thin sheets and different shapes. Aluminum can be hammered into a thin sheet and into the shape of a pot or pan.

- Metals are **ductile**. They can be made into thin wires. Most of the wires in electrical appliances are made of metals.

- Some metals allow electricity to flow through them easily. These metals are good conductors of electricity. Electricity flows easily through wires made of copper.

- Most metals are good conductors of heat. They allow heat to flow easily through them. This is the reason why radiators, pots, pans, and irons are made of metals.

◀ **Figure 3-27** Metals can be hammered into different shapes.

2 LIST: What are three properties of metals?

Properties of Nonmetals Elements that lack most of the properties of a metal are called **nonmetals**, so they look dull. Most solid nonmetals are brittle. They are easily broken. They cannot be pounded into different shapes or pulled into thin wires. Nonmetals are poor conductors of electricity and heat. Nonmetallic elements may exist at room temperature as solids, liquids, or gases.

Nonmetals are very useful elements. For example, phosphorus is used in matches. Sulfur is used to make rubber. Nonmetals are also important to all living things in other ways. The nonmetals nitrogen and oxygen are found in the air that we breathe. Nitrogen helps organisms to make proteins. Most organisms need oxygen to breathe.

▲ **Figure 3-28** Matches and rubber are made from nonmetals.

3 RELATE: Why do nonmetals look dull?

✓ CHECKING CONCEPTS

1. Elements to the right of the zigzag line in the periodic table are _____.

2. Metals can be hammered into thin sheets because they are _____.

3. It is possible to make copper wire because copper is _____.

4. Most _____ are good conductors of heat.

5. Nonmetals are _____ conductors of heat and electricity.

6. The nonmetal _____ is used in matches.

THINKING CRITICALLY

7. **IDENTIFY:** What two properties of metals make them useful materials for the electrical wiring in your home?

8. **INFER:** What property of metals allows a jeweler to hammer a piece of silver to make jewelry?

9. **CLASSIFY:** Use the periodic table on pages 66 and 67 to identify the following elements as metals or nonmetals.

   a. Zinc   **e.** Selenium

   b. Sulfur   **f.** Magnesium

   c. Xenon   **g.** Platinum

   d. Potassium   **h.** Phosphorus

DESIGNING AN EXPERIMENT

Design an experiment to solve the following problem. Include a hypothesis, variables, a procedure, and a type of data to study.

PROBLEM: Element x is an unidentified element. Is it a metal or a nonmetal?

Hands-On Activity

COMPARING METALS AND NONMETALS

You will need safety goggles, an electrical conductivity tester, a 5- to 6-cm piece of uninsulated copper wire, graphite from a mechanical pencil, a paper clip, and a small block of wood.

1. Compare a piece of uninsulated copper wire to a piece of graphite from a mechanical pencil. Note the luster of both samples.

2. Put on safety goggles. Check for ductility. Bend the copper wire, the piece of graphite, a paper clip, and a block of wood as far as possible. Note changes in each of the samples.

3. Check for electrical conductivity. Touch the free ends of the wires in the electrical conductivity tester to each other. Make sure that the light bulb goes on. Next touch the ends of the wires to the ends of the uninsulated copper wire. Observe any changes to the light bulb. Do the same for the paper clip, the graphite, and the block of wood. Note any changes to the light bulb.

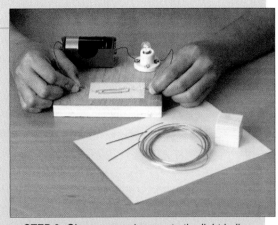

▲ **STEP 3** Observe any changes to the light bulb.

Practicing Your Skills

4. **COMPARE:** What are the properties of the copper wire compared to the properties of the graphite from the mechanical pencil?

5. **DESCRIBE:** Which of the four samples conducted electricity? How do you know?

3-9 What are the halogens and the noble gases?

Objectives

Locate the halogens and the `noble gases on the periodic table. Identify the properties of the halogens and the noble gases.

Key Terms

halogens: elements that make up Group 17 in the periodic table

noble gases: elements that make up Group 18 in the periodic table

The Halogens Group 17 in the periodic table contains the five elements that make up the **halogens**. These elements—fluorine, chlorine, bromine, iodine, and astatine—have a similar atomic structure. The halogens can vary their physical states from solid to gas at room temperature. They can also change color when changing state. For example, bromine is a red-brown liquid that becomes a red gas at room temperature. Iodine is a gray-black solid that can become a blue-violet gas.

The halogens can also be quite dangerous. However, when they combine with other elements, they can form matter that is very useful. For example, chlorine combines with sodium to form table salt. Fluorine combines with other elements to form products that prevent tooth decay. Matter made with iodine can be used to help prevent

HALOGENS		
Element	**Symbol**	**Uses**
Fluorine	Fl	Prevents tooth decay
Chlorine	Cl	Purifies water
Bromine	Br	Used in photographic film
Iodine	I	Prevents infection
Astatine	At	Used in halogen lights

▲ **Figure 3-29** The halogens can be found in Group 17 in the periodic table.

infections in wounds. Figure 3-29 lists the halogens.

▷ 1 **LIST:** Name the five halogens.

The Noble Gases Look at Group 18 of the periodic table on page 67. What do the elements in Group 18 have in common? The six elements in the last group of the periodic table are gases. They are called the **noble gases**. All of these elements have similar properties and atomic structure.

In the past, these elements were also called inert gases. The word *inert* means "inactive." At one time, these elements were thought to occur naturally as pure substances. Pure substances that occur naturally do not interact with other substances. However, scientists have discovered that noble gases can be forced to combine with other elements, such as fluorine.

▷ 2 **DEFINE:** What is a noble gas?

Familiar Noble Gases The six noble gases are helium, neon, argon, krypton, xenon, and radon. The names of some of the noble gases may be familiar to you. You have probably heard of helium and neon. If you have heard of kryptonite, krypton is not related to it. In fact, kryptonite, which is mentioned in fictional tales, is not a real substance. All the noble gases are found in small amounts in Earth's atmosphere. Of all the noble gases, argon is the most plentiful. It makes up about 1% of the atmosphere. The names and chemical symbols of the six noble gases are listed in Figure 3-30.

NOBLE GASES		
Element	**Symbol**	**Uses**
Helium	He	Fills balloons
Neon	Ne	Lighting
Argon	Ar	Lighting
Krypton	Kr	Lighting
Xenon	Xe	Lighting
Radon	Rn	None

▲ **Figure 3-30** The noble gases can be found in Group 18 in the periodic table.

▷ 3 **LIST:** Name the six noble gases.

Uses of Noble Gases Most of the noble gases have many important uses. Neon is used in lights because it gives off a bright red glow when electricity passes through it. By mixing neon with other gases, different colors can be produced. Helium is used to fill balloons and xenon is used in photographic lamps.

▲ **Figure 3-31** Neon is used in lights.

 EXPLAIN: What is helium used for?

1. Where are the halogens located in the periodic table?
2. Where are the noble gases located in the periodic table?
3. What is the meaning of inert?
4. Which noble gas makes up about 1% of Earth's atmosphere?

💡 **THINKING CRITICALLY**

5. **STATE:** Why were noble gases once called inert gases?
6. **ANALYZE:** Why do you think neon is used in signs?

BUILDING LANGUAGE ARTS SKILLS

Researching Noble gases are so named because of nobles. Look up the word *noble* in a dictionary, an encyclopedia, or on the Internet. Find out how noble gases are related to nobles.

 Real-Life Science

BLIMPS

Have you ever looked up into the sky and seen a blimp passing by? A blimp is a type of airship that is lifted into the air by the noble gas helium. Helium not only lifts a blimp high into the sky, it also gives a blimp its shape. The baglike body of a blimp, called the envelope, does not have structure unless helium fills it.

▲ **Figure 3-32** Blimps are airships that are filled with the noble gas helium.

Helium is used to lift blimps because helium is lighter than air and it will not burn in air. At one time, hydrogen gas was used to fill airships. Hydrogen is lighter than helium. However, on May 6, 1937, the largest airship ever built, the Hindenburg, burst into flames over Lakehurst, New Jersey. Since hydrogen was used to lift and fill the Hindenburg, it was no longer considered safe to use.

Today, blimps are used to advertise certain products and to transport photographic equipment to film special events. In some countries, they are used in military operations.

Thinking Critically Hydrogen is lighter than helium. Why is hydrogen not used to lift blimps instead of helium?

3-10 What are isotopes?

Objectives

Explain what an isotope of an element is.
Compare the three isotopes of hydrogen.

Key Term

isotope (EYE-suh-tohp)**:** atom of an element with the same number of protons as the other atoms but a different number of neutrons

Different Atomic Masses The atomic number of an element never changes. All atoms of the same element have the same number of protons in their nuclei. However, all atoms of the same element may not have the same number of neutrons in their nuclei. This means that atoms of the same element can have different atomic masses. The difference in atomic mass is caused by a different number of neutrons in the nuclei of the atoms of an element.

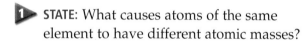 **STATE:** What causes atoms of the same element to have different atomic masses?

Isotopes Atoms of the same element that have different atomic masses are called isotopes. **Isotopes** are atoms of an element that have the same number of protons as the other atoms of the element but a different number of neutrons in their nuclei.

Although the number of neutrons in the atoms of an element may be different, atoms are always identified by the number of protons. For example, there are several isotopes of the element copper. One of the isotopes has 36 neutrons in the nuclei of its atoms. Another isotope has 34 neutrons in the nuclei of its atoms. Because both of these isotopes have 29 protons in the nuclei of their atoms, they are both atoms of the element copper.

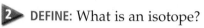 **DEFINE:** What is an isotope?

Atomic Mass The atomic mass for each element can be found in the periodic table. The atomic mass given for each element is actually an average of the atomic masses of all the isotopes of that element. This explains why an element's atomic mass is not a whole number.

EXPLAIN: What does the atomic mass for each element actually represent?

Isotopes of Common Elements Hydrogen has three isotopes. The three isotopes of hydrogen are known as protium (PROHT-ee-uhm), deuterium (doo-TIR-ee-uhm), and tritium (TRIHT-ee-uhm). These isotopes of hydrogen are also called hydrogen-1 (H-1), hydrogen-2 (H-2), and hydrogen-3 (H-3). The numbers 1, 2, and 3 represent the mass numbers of each of the isotopes. An atom of protium (H-1) has only one proton and no neutrons in its nucleus. An atom of deuterium (H-2) has one proton and one neutron. An atom of tritium (H-3) has one proton and two neutrons.

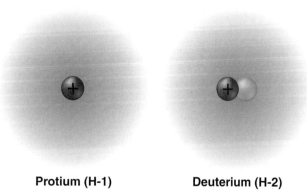

Protium (H-1)
atom

Deuterium (H-2)
atom

Tritium (H-3)
atom

◀ **Figure 3-33**
The three isotopes
of hydrogen

All elements have two or more isotopes. Carbon-12 and carbon-14 are two isotopes of the element carbon. These isotopes are also written as C-12 and C-14. Boron-10 (B-10) and boron-11 (B-11) are isotopes of the element boron. Two important isotopes of uranium are uranium-235 (U-235) and uranium-238 (U-238).

 LIST: What are the three isotopes of hydrogen called?

✓ CHECKING CONCEPTS

1. What causes some atoms of the same element to have different atomic masses?
2. In the periodic table, where can the atomic mass of an element be found?
3. What identifies an atom of an element?
4. How many neutrons are there in an atom of protium? Deuterium? Tritium?

 THINKING CRITICALLY

5. **EXPLAIN:** Why is the atomic mass of an element not a whole number?

6. **CALCULATE:** The atomic number of carbon is 6. How many protons and neutrons are there in an atom of carbon-12? Of carbon-14?
7. **ANALYZE:** The mass number of oxygen is 16. Its atomic mass is 15.999. The atomic number of oxygen is 8. Which of the following statements about the isotopes of oxygen are true? Why?
   a. All of the isotopes have eight neutrons.
   b. All of the isotopes have eight neutrons or more.
   c. Some of the isotopes have fewer than eight neutrons.
   d. All of the isotopes have fewer than eight neutrons.

INTERPRETING VISUALS

Use Figure 3-33 to answer the following questions.

8. **ANALYZE:** Which isotope contains two neutrons in its nucleus?
9. **IDENTIFY:** Which atom has the largest nucleus?
10. **INFER:** What is the atomic number of each isotope?
11. **INFER:** Which isotope has the smallest atomic mass?

Integrating Life Science

TOPIC: cells

KILLING CANCER CELLS

The human body is made up of trillions of cells. Cells divide and organize themselves to keep the body healthy. They can also replace themselves to promote repair. Cancer occurs when cells cannot control their growth and development. Cancer cells divide, multiply, and spread. These cells can also invade organs. As they invade organs, they damage healthy cells and send out substances that weaken the body.

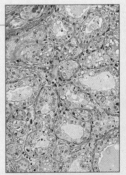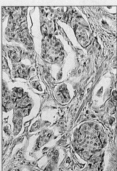

▲ **Figure 3-34** Healthy cells (left) and cancerous cells (right)

Research scientists have uncovered different ways to treat different types of cancer. Radiation therapy is one method. One type of radiation therapy uses radioactive isotopes to kill cancer cells. This type of treatment places radioactive isotopes close to the cancer cells. The high-energy rays from the isotopes attack the cancer cells. Some radioactive isotopes used in this type of therapy are radium-223, gallium-67, iodine-123, and fluorine-18.

Thinking Critically How are radioactive isotopes used to treat certain types of cancer?

LAB ACTIVITY
Investigating the Modern Model of the Atom

Materials

2 Targets
1 Sheet of carbon paper
4 Paper clips
1 Marble
Chair

BACKGROUND

Over the past 100 years, the model of the atom has gone through several changes. Our current understanding is that protons and neutrons are found in the atom's center, the nucleus. The electrons are found in an electron cloud. An electron cloud is an area where each electron is most likely to be found. It surrounds the nucleus of an atom.

PURPOSE

In this activity, you will use a target as a model to investigate the nucleus and the electron cloud of an atom according to the modern theory of the atom.

PROCEDURE

1. Copy the chart in Figure 3-36.

2. Place a sheet of carbon paper between two targets with the shiny side facing the bottom target as shown in Figure 3-35. The circles represent energy levels of the "atom," while the bull's-eye represents the nucleus. A marble striking the top target will make a mark on the bottom target. Fasten targets and carbon paper together with a paper clip at each corner.

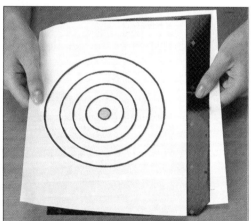

▲ **Figure 3-35** Target

Marble-Drops on Target	Observations
Number of marble-drops on bull's-eye	
Number of marble-drops on circle 1	
Number of marble-drops on circle 2	
Number of marble-drops on circle 3	
Number of marble-drops on circle 4	

▲ **Figure 3-36** Copy this chart and use it to record your observations.

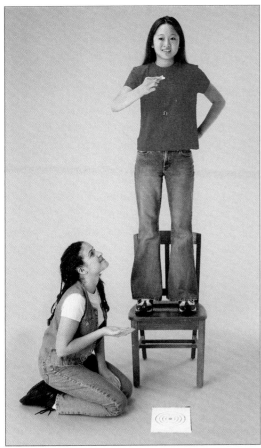

▲ STEP 4 Drop the marble on the target.

3. Carefully stand on a chair with the marble in your hand. Extend your arm so that it is about 2 m above the floor.

4. Have a partner place the targets directly below your hand. Drop the marble on the target. Your partner must catch the marble on the first bounce. If it is not caught, there will be more than one mark for each marble drop.

5. Repeat 50 times. The spots on the back of the target indicate places where the marble was dropped.

6. Switch roles with your partner and drop the marble another 50 times. Record your results.

▲ STEP 5 Spots on the target show where the marble was dropped.

CONCLUSIONS

1. **OBSERVE:** Describe what your bottom target looks like.

2. **MODEL:** What do the marble-drops on the target represent?

3. **COMPARE:** Do you expect the other groups to get the same pattern? Explain your answer.

4. **INFER:** How might this experiment help to explain the modern theory of an atom?

5. **ANALYZE:** The atomic model proposed by Niels Bohr states that electrons are found in energy levels much like planets moving in orbits around the Sun. How is the electron cloud different from the orbits of planets moving around the Sun?

Chapter Summary

Lesson 3-1
- **Elements** are substances that cannot be chemically broken down into simpler substances.

Lesson 3-2
- An **atom** is the smallest part of an element that can be identified as that element.

Lesson 3-3
- Atoms are made up of **protons**, **neutrons**, and **electrons**.

Lesson 3-4
- The **atomic number** of an element is the number of protons in the nucleus of an atom of that element.

Lesson 3-5
- The total mass of the protons and neutrons in an atom is the **atomic mass** of that atom.
- The **mass number** of an element is equal to the number of protons and neutrons in the nucleus of an atom of that element.

Lesson 3-6
- Electrons are arranged in **energy levels** around the nucleus of an atom.

Lesson 3-7
- In the modern periodic table, elements are arranged in order of increasing atomic number.

Lesson 3-8
- A zigzag line on the periodic table separates the **metals** from the **nonmetals**.

Lesson 3-9
- The **halogens** are the five elements in Group 17 in the periodic table.
- The **noble gases** are the six elements in Group 18 in the periodic table.

Lesson 3-10
- Atoms of the same element that have different numbers of neutrons are called **isotopes**.

Key Term Challenges

atom (p. 54)
atomic mass (p. 60)
atomic number (p. 58)
chemical symbol (p. 64)
ductile (p. 68)
electron (p. 56)
element (p. 52)
energy level (p. 62)
group (p. 64)
halogens (p. 70)
isotope (p. 72)
luster (p. 68)
malleable (p. 68)
mass number (p. 60)
metal (p. 68)
neutron (p. 56)
noble gases (p. 70)
nonmetal (p. 68)
nucleus (p. 56)
period (p. 64)
periodic (p. 64)
proton (p. 56)

MATCHING Write the Key Term from above that best matches each description.

1. number of protons and neutrons in the nucleus of an atom
2. particle in an atom that has a negative charge
3. number of protons in the nucleus of an atom
4. smallest part of an element that can be identified as that element
5. particle in the nucleus of an atom that does not have any charge
6. has the same number of protons but a different number of neutrons

FILL IN Write the Key Term from above that best completes each statement.

7. The _____ are found in Group 18 of the periodic table.
8. A repeating pattern is _____.
9. The center, or core, of an atom is called the _____.
10. There are more than 100 known _____.
11. An _____ is the place in the electron cloud where electrons are most likely to be found.
12. There are 18 columns or _____ on the periodic table.

Content Challenges TEST PREP

MULTIPLE CHOICE Write the letter of the term or phrase that best completes each statement.

1. In the early 1800s, an atomic theory of matter was developed by
   a. Democritus.
   b. Dalton.
   c. Rutherford.
   d. Thomson.

2. The first scientist to suggest that atoms contain smaller particles was
   a. Thomson.
   b. Rutherford.
   c. Bohr.
   d. Dalton.

3. Rutherford pictured atoms as being made mostly of
   a. empty space.
   b. positively charged material.
   c. electrons.
   d. the nucleus.

4. Rutherford's model of the atom included
   a. a small central core.
   b. a positive material filled with electrons.
   c. energy levels for electrons.
   d. neutrons.

5. Niels Bohr proposed that electrons
   a. orbit the nucleus.
   b. are inside the nucleus.
   c. do not exist.
   d. cannot be located exactly in an atom.

6. If an electron gains enough energy,
   a. it jumps to a higher energy level.
   b. it falls to a lower energy level.
   c. it gives off light.
   d. it falls into the nucleus.

7. The atomic number of an atom is equal to
   a. the number of protons and neutrons.
   b. the number of electrons and neutrons.
   c. the number of protons.
   d. the number of protons and electrons.

8. The letters *amu* stand for
   a. atomic measuring unit.
   b. alternate mass unit.
   c. atomic mass unit.
   d. atomic matter unit.

9. Tritium is an
   a. electron energy level.
   b. isotope of hydrogen.
   c. element with atomic number 102.
   d. isotope of carbon.

10. Argon and krypton are
    a. metals.
    b. protons.
    c. neutrons.
    d. noble gases.

TRUE/FALSE Write *true* if the statement is true. If the statement is false, change the underlined term to make the statement true.

11. An isotope of an element has the same number of protons but a different number of <u>electrons</u>.

12. The second energy level can hold <u>eight</u> electrons.

13. Scientists <u>can</u> predict the exact location of an electron in an atom.

14. The number of protons and <u>electrons</u> in a neutral atom must be equal.

Concept Challenges

WRITTEN RESPONSE **Answer each of the following questions in complete sentences.**

1. **EXPLAIN:** How did Dalton come to the conclusion that matter is made up of atoms?

2. **COMPARE:** In what ways did Dalton, Thomson, and Rutherford have similar ideas about atoms? In what ways did their ideas differ?

3. **ANALYZE:** Why is the atomic mass of an element not a whole number, whereas the mass number is always a whole number?

4. **PREDICT:** How many electrons would be found in the second energy level of an atom of nitrogen, which has an atomic number of 7?

5. **COMPARE:** How are metals different from nonmetals?

INTERPRETING A DIAGRAM **Use Figure 3-37 to answer the following questions.**

6. How many electrons are in an atom of element *x*?

7. How many electrons are in the first energy level in an atom of element *x*?

8. How many protons are in an atom of element *x*?

9. If there are 18 neutrons in an atom of element *x*, what is the mass number of an atom of element *x*?

10. Use the periodic table on pages 66 and 67 to identify element *x*.

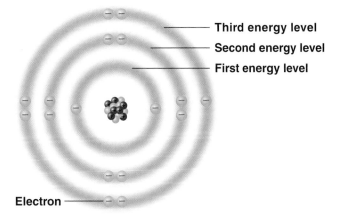

Third energy level
Second energy level
First energy level

Electron

▲ **Figure 3-37** Element *x*

Chapter 4 Compounds and Mixtures

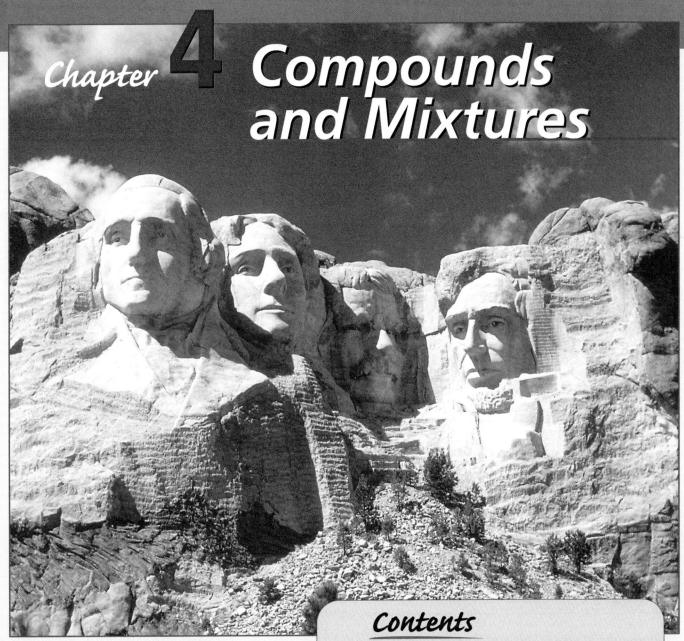

▲ **Figure 4-1** Mount Rushmore, South Dakota

Can you recognize the four faces carved in Figure 4-1? The faces are those of George Washington, Thomas Jefferson, Theodore Roosevelt, and Abraham Lincoln—four American presidents. The memorial is carved out of granite. Granite is a hard rock that is actually made up of other types of matter. Granite keeps the properties of the different types of matter that it is made up of.

▶Why do you think the memorial is carved out of granite?

Contents

4-1 What are three types of matter?

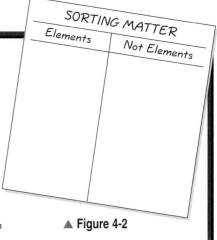
Objective

Describe similarities and differences among elements, compounds, and mixtures.

Key Terms

element: substance that cannot be chemically broken down into simpler substances

compound: substance made up of two or more elements that are chemically combined

mixture: two or more substances that have been physically combined

substance: any element or compound

Organizing Matter You may have items that you like to collect, such as rocks, stamps, sea glass, or baseball cards. If you do, you may sort your collection based on different or similar characteristics, such as size, shape, date, or team. Kinds of matter can be sorted, too. Just like you might sort your collection based on one characteristic, matter can be organized, or classified, into three groups based on the makeup of the matter.

▶ **LIST:** What are some of the ways to organize a collection?

Elements, Compounds, and Mixtures Matter can be classified into three main types—elements, compounds, and mixtures. You have learned that an **element** is made up of only one kind of atom. For example, pure gold is always made up of

atoms that contain 79 protons. A **compound** is made up of atoms of two or more elements that are chemically combined. The elements in a given compound are always combined in a fixed ratio. For example, every particle of the compound baking soda is made up of one atom of sodium, one atom of hydrogen, one atom of carbon, and three atoms of oxygen.

A **mixture** is made up of two or more kinds of matter that are physically combined, or mixed together. The kinds of matter in a mixture can be present in any amounts. A mixture of sugar and cinnamon can contain any amount of sugar and any amount of cinnamon.

▲ **Figure 4-3** Examples of the three main types of matter

▶ **IDENTIFY:** What are the three main types of matter?

Substances Elements and compounds share a similar characteristic. Every sample of an element has the same exact properties as every other sample. Similarly, all samples of a given compound have the same exact properties as every other sample of that compound. For example, the copper used to make a teakettle will have the same properties as the copper used to make an electric wire. A sample of pure sugar, a compound used to sweeten coffee, will be identical to a sample of pure sugar used to make candy. Because they share this characteristic, elements and compounds are classified as substances. A **substance** is any element or compound.

 DEFINE: What is a substance?

✓ CHECKING CONCEPTS

1. Matter is classified into three groups based on the _____ of the matter.

2. An _____ is made up of only one kind of atom.

3. A _____ is made up of atoms of different elements that are chemically combined.

4. The elements in a given compound are always combined in a _____ ratio.

5. A _____ is made up of two or more different kinds of matter that are physically combined.

6. The amounts of the different kinds of matter in a _____ can vary.

7. A _____ is any element or compound.

💡 THINKING CRITICALLY

8. **ANALYZE:** A sample of matter is made up of three different atoms that are chemically combined. What type of matter is it? How do you know?

9. **HYPOTHESIZE:** A substance is made up of two atoms of oxygen. Is it an element or a compound? How do you know?

Web InfoSearch

Properties Substances can be recognized by their physical and chemical properties. These properties can be labeled as *extensive properties* and *intensive properties*. Extensive properties include weight and mass. Intensive properties include melting point and boiling point.

SEARCH: Use the Internet to find out more about these types of properties. List other intensive and extensive properties. Start your search at www.conceptsandchallenges.com. Some key search words are **intensive properties** and **extensive properties.**

⚛ *People in Science*

ROBERT BOYLE (1627–1691)

The Irish-born scientist Robert Boyle was the first scientist to establish the scientific method of experimentation to test hypotheses. He questioned the early belief that materials were made up of four elements—earth, air, fire, and water. He believed that the basic elements of matter were "corpuscles." These corpuscles, or particles, could be found in various types and sizes, and could arrange themselves into groups called mixtures and compounds. Robert Boyle also showed that the properties of a compound are different from those of the particles that it is made up of.

▲ **Figure 4-4** Robert Boyle

Robert Boyle contributed a vast amount of knowledge to the scientific world. His work with gases and pressure led to Boyle's law. He is also credited with the invention of the match.

Thinking Critically Robert Boyle believed that the basic elements of matter were corpuscles. What would a modern scientist call these basic elements of matter?

4-2 What is a compound?

Objectives
Explain that a compound is made up of two or more elements. Describe how chemical bonds form new substances.

Key Terms
molecule: smallest part of a substance that has all the properties of that substance
chemical bond: force of attraction that holds atoms together

Combining Elements An element can combine with other elements to form a new substance called a compound. A compound is a substance made up of two or more elements that are chemically combined. For example, hydrogen and oxygen are elements. They are both gases with very different properties at room temperature. When these two elements chemically combine, they can form two different compounds that are liquids at room temperature. You are familiar with one of these compounds. It is water. The other compound is hydrogen peroxide, a substance used to clean cuts.

1 EXPLAIN: What is a compound?

Common Compounds Sugar is a compound. It is made of carbon, hydrogen, and oxygen. Table salt is a compound, too. It is made of the elements sodium and chlorine. You may be familiar with some of the compounds listed in Figure 4-5.

SOME COMMON COMPOUNDS	
Compound	**Elements**
Sand	Silicon, oxygen
Hydrogen peroxide	Hydrogen, oxygen
Chalk	Calcium, carbon, oxygen
Rust	Iron, oxygen

▲ Figure 4-5

2 NAME: What elements are in chalk?

Properties of Compounds The properties of a compound are very different from the properties of the elements that make it up. Some elements that make up a compound may be dangerous. But a compound formed from these elements may be relatively harmless. For example, sodium is a very active metal. Chlorine is a yellow, poisonous gas. When combined, these elements make up the compound sodium chloride, or table salt.

▲ **Figure 4-6** The active metal sodium (left) chemically combines with the poisonous gas chlorine (right) to form table salt.

3 CONTRAST: What are the properties of sodium, chlorine, and sodium chloride?

Molecules Most compounds are made of molecules. A **molecule** is the smallest part of a substance that has all the properties of that substance. A molecule can be a single atom or may be made up of a great many atoms. For example, a molecule of iron is a single iron atom. A molecule of sucrose, a type of sugar, is made up of 45 atoms.

Silicon dioxide is a compound found in sand. It is made of the elements silicon and oxygen. One molecule of silicon dioxide is made from one atom of silicon and two atoms of oxygen. A single molecule of silicon dioxide has all the properties of silicon dioxide. Just as all the atoms of an element are alike, all the molecules of a compound are alike.

4 DEFINE: What is a molecule?

Breaking Down Compounds A compound is formed as a result of a chemical change. The elements in a compound combine by forming chemical bonds between the atoms. A **chemical bond** is the force of attraction that holds atoms in a molecule together. Atoms bond together to form molecules. When bonding occurs, a new substance with its own properties is formed.

A chemical change can also cause the molecules that make up a compound to break down into simpler substances. In order to break the molecules down, the chemical bonds holding the atoms together have to be broken. Heating a compound is one way to break it down. When sugar is heated, it melts. If the melted sugar is heated long enough, hydrogen and oxygen enter the air in the form of water vapor. Finally, only a black solid remains. This solid is the element carbon. So, heating sugar can cause it to break down into water, containing hydrogen and oxygen, and carbon. These are the elements that make up sugar.

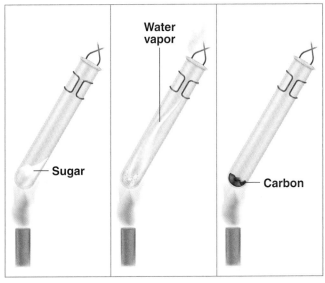

▲ **Figure 4-7** Heating sugar can break it down into simpler substances.

Another way to break down a compound is by using electricity. Scientists working in laboratories can obtain hydrogen gas and oxygen gas by passing electricity through a sample of slightly acidic water.

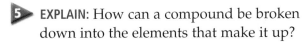 **EXPLAIN:** How can a compound be broken down into the elements that make it up?

✔ **CHECKING CONCEPTS**

1. A compound is made up of two or more _____ .

2. The compound _____ is made up of the elements hydrogen, oxygen, and carbon.

3. The properties of a compound are _____ from the properties of the elements that form it.

4. A _____ is the smallest part of a substance that has all the properties of that substance.

5. A compound is formed as a result of a _____ .

6. A _____ is the force of attraction that holds atoms together.

7. Using heat and electricity can _____ a compound into the elements that make up the compound.

THINKING CRITICALLY

8. **INFER:** A recipe calls for a cup of sugar to be heated slowly over a low flame. What could happen if the sugar is heated over a high flame?

9. **HYPOTHESIZE:** When an unknown solid is heated, two different gases and a liquid are formed. Is the solid a compound or an element? How do you know?

10. **ANALYZE:** How is a molecule different from an atom?

HEALTH AND SAFETY TIP

The compound carbon monoxide is a deadly gas. It is difficult to detect because it is odorless and colorless. Carbon monoxide can be produced by the incomplete burning of fuels in cars and in heating furnaces. If it is inhaled in small amounts, it can cause people to feel sleepy. If it is inhaled in large amounts, it can cause death. Why do you think having a carbon monoxide detector in your home is a good idea?

4-3 What is a mixture?

Separating a Mixture
HANDS-ON ACTIVITY

1. Place one-half cup of iron-fortified cereal into a plastic sandwich bag. Squeeze as much air out of the bag as you can. Seal the plastic bag.

2. Use your hands to crush the cereal into a fine powder. Then, pour the cereal into a bowl. Add enough water to the bowl to completely cover the cereal.

3. Cover one end of a magnet with plastic wrap and use it to stir the mixture for at least 10 minutes. Remove the magnet and let the liquid on the magnet drain back into the bowl.

4. Hold the magnet over a sheet of white paper. Use a hand lens to observe the particles on the end of the magnet.

THINK ABOUT IT: What did you observe on the end of the magnet? Where did the matter come from?

STEP 3

Objective
Describe the physical properties of a mixture.

Mixtures Cut up some tomatoes, lettuce, onions, and green peppers. Put the pieces in a bowl and stir them together. What do you have? Some people would say that you have a salad. A scientist might say that you have a mixture. You have learned that a mixture is made up of two or more substances that are physically combined. Each part of a mixture keeps its own properties.

Not all mixtures are as easy to identify. If you put some salt in a glass of water and stir, you would have a mixture of salt and water. But this mixture is different from the salad mixture. You cannot see the individual parts of salt or water.

1 CONTRAST: What is the difference between a salad mixture and a salt-water mixture?

Kinds of Mixtures The kinds of matter in a mixture can be present in varying amounts. The discussion above describes the two basic types of mixtures—evenly mixed and unevenly mixed. The mixture of salt and water is evenly mixed. You cannot see the individual particles of salt or water. The salt is still salt, and the water is still water. However, they are so evenly mixed that every part of this mixture is exactly the same as every other part. A drop taken from the top of the mixture will be identical to a drop taken from the bottom.

The salad is unevenly mixed. One part of the salad may have more tomato while another part has more green pepper. Each part of the mixture keeps its own properties. A tomato is still red and tastes like a tomato.

▲ **Figure 4-8** A salad is a mixture. Each part of the mixture keeps its own properties.

2 INFER: Why do the different kinds of matter in a mixture keep their own properties?

Separating a Mixture The properties of the different kinds of matter in a mixture can be used to separate the mixture. Because the parts of a mixture are not chemically combined, they can be separated by physical means. For example, each of the different vegetables could be picked out of the salad by hand.

A physical property of water is that it evaporates when it is heated. So, if you heat a mixture of salt and water, the water will evaporate and the salt will be left behind. The mixture will be separated. Some mixtures can be separated by filtering. If a mixture of sand and water is poured into a filter, the water will pass through. The sand will be trapped by the filter.

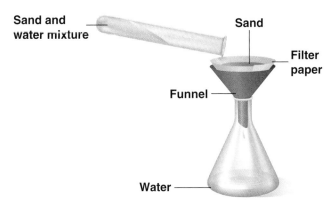

Sand and water mixture

Sand

Filter paper

Funnel

Water

▲ Figure 4-9 Separating a mixture of sand and water

 EXPLAIN: How can you separate a mixture of sand and water?

☑ CHECKING CONCEPTS

1. Salt water is an example of a _____.
2. The substances in a mixture are _____ combined.

3. The substances in a mixture can be present in _____ amount.

4. The substances in a mixture always keep their own _____.

5. The substances in a mixture can be _____ by using the physical properties of the substances.

6. A mixture of _____ and water can be separated by filtering the mixture.

THINKING CRITICALLY

7. **HYPOTHESIZE:** Will freezing a mixture of salt and water separate the two substances? Explain your answer.

8. **CLASSIFY:** A teaspoon of instant coffee is placed in a cup of boiling water. Is this a mixture or a compound? Explain your answer.

DESIGNING AN EXPERIMENT

Design an experiment to solve the following problem. Include a hypothesis, variables, a procedure, and a type of data to study.

PROBLEM: You have a mixture of sand, water, and gravel. How can you separate this mixture into its different parts?

 Real-Life Science

MIXTURES THAT YOU CAN EAT

Have you ever gone camping or hiking and taken some trail mix with you? As the name of this snack tells you, trail mix is a mixture. You can see the individual bits of dried fruits and nuts. You could pick out the individual parts with your fingers if you wanted to.

Think about some of the other foods that you eat every day. Many of these foods are mixtures. Rice and beans, vegetable soup, ice cream—all are mixtures.

Thinking Critically If you were to make trail mix, do you have to follow the recipe exactly?

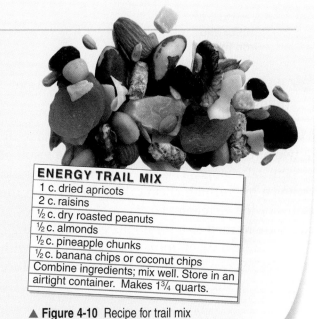

ENERGY TRAIL MIX
1 c. dried apricots
2 c. raisins
½ c. dry roasted peanuts
½ c. almonds
½ c. pineapple chunks
½ c. banana chips or coconut chips
Combine ingredients; mix well. Store in an airtight container. Makes 1¾ quarts.

▲ Figure 4-10 Recipe for trail mix

4-4 How are mixtures and compounds different?

Objective

Contrast the properties of mixtures with the properties of compounds.

Making a Mixture The different kinds of matter in a mixture are physically combined. A fruit salad is a mixture of different kinds of fruit. You can make a mixture of iron filings and sulfur by mixing the two substances together.

Iron filings are magnetic slivers of gray metal. Sulfur is a nonmetallic yellow powder. Just like each piece of fruit in a salad keeps its properties, each substance in the iron-sulfur mixture will keep its own properties. You would be able to see the grains of yellow powder and slivers of gray metal in a mixture of these two substances.

Iron filings

Sulfur

◀ Figure 4-11
Making a mixture of sulfur and iron

A mixture of sulfur and iron filings

▶ 1 INFER: How can you make a mixture of iron filings and sulfur?

Making a Compound A compound is made up of two or more elements. It is formed as a result of a chemical change. The elements in a compound combine by forming chemical bonds between the atoms of the elements. For example, molecules of sugar are formed as a result of a chemical change. Atoms of hydrogen form chemical bonds with atoms of oxygen and atoms of carbon to produce molecules of sugar.

Not only can iron and sulfur be physically combined to make a mixture, they can also be chemically combined to form a compound. This compound is called iron sulfide. Iron sulfide forms when a mixture of iron filings and sulfur is heated. The atoms of the two elements will combine to form chemical bonds with each other. The compound iron sulfide will be produced. Like all compounds, the properties of iron sulfide are different from the properties of the elements that make it up.

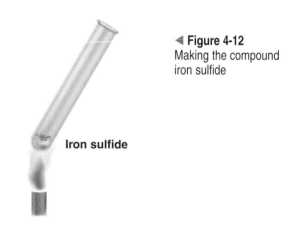

◀ Figure 4-12
Making the compound iron sulfide

Iron sulfide

▶ 2 EXPLAIN: What happens when a mixture of iron filings and sulfur is heated?

Comparing Mixtures and Compounds Mixtures and compounds are different in several ways. A mixture of iron and sulfur does not have a definite chemical composition. The mixture might contain equal parts of each element. Or, it might have twice as much of one element as the other. Each substance in a mixture of iron and sulfur keeps its own properties. A mixture of iron and sulfur can be separated by physical means. For example, a magnet can be used to attract the iron.

The compound iron sulfide always has a definite chemical composition. Every molecule of iron sulfide contains one atom of iron and one atom of sulfur.

When elements combine chemically, each element loses its properties. The iron and sulfur in iron sulfide cannot be separated by physical means. Figure 4-13 lists some differences between mixtures and compounds.

COMPARING MIXTURES AND COMPOUNDS	
Mixtures	Compounds
Made of two or more substances physically combined	Made of two or more substances chemically combined
Substances keep their own properties	Substances lose their own properties
Can be separated by physical means	Can be separated only by chemical means
Have no definite chemical composition	Have a definite chemical composition

▲ **Figure 4-13** Differences between mixtures and compounds

 CONTRAST: How are mixtures and compounds different?

✔ **CHECKING CONCEPTS**

1. The elements in a _____ are chemically combined.
2. Each kind of matter in a _____ keeps its own properties.
3. A _____ does not have a definite chemical composition.
4. A _____ cannot be separated by physical means.

 THINKING CRITICALLY

5. **INFER:** When a certain poisonous gas is combined with a chemically active metal, a fine white powdery substance results. The new substance is neither poisonous nor chemically active. Is the powder a mixture or a compound? How do you know?
6. **COMPARE:** Water is a compound. Salt water is a mixture. List the differences between water and salt water.

Integrating Earth Science

TOPICS: rocks, minerals

CLASSIFYING ROCKS

Like other types of matter, rocks can be classified as elements, compounds, or mixtures. Some rocks are actually made of pure elements. For example, copper and gold are elements that can be found in nearly pure form. However, rocks that are mixtures of different compounds are more common than are rocks made of pure elements.

Some compounds that can be found in certain rocks include quartz, mica, and feldspar. Quartz is a hard, cloudy-looking rock that is actually a compound made up of silicon and oxygen. One form of mica is a black compound made up of the elements potassium, aluminum, silicon, oxygen, and hydrogen. Feldspar is a milky-white or pink compound that can be made up of aluminum, silicon, sodium, potassium, or calcium and oxygen. A mixture of these three compounds can be found in a type of rock called granite. Granite is a hard rock with big grains of quartz, mica, and feldspar.

Thinking Critically How would you classify granite?

▲ **Figure 4-14** Granite is a mixture.

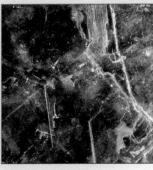
▲ **Figure 4-15** Mica can be found in granite.

LAB ACTIVITY
Separating Mixtures

Materials
Safety goggles
Lab apron, plastic gloves
Sand
Epsom salt
Sawdust, iron filings
2 Clear plastic cups
Teaspoons, stirrers
Water
Magnet
Plastic wrap
Paper towels
2 Beakers
Fine sieve, filter paper

▲ STEP 3 Make a sand and Epsom salt mixture.

▲ STEP 5 Obtain a cup of water to pour into the mixture.

BACKGROUND

Mixtures surround you. Everything from salt water in the ocean to your bowl of morning cereal, mixtures are part of our everyday lives. Salt water and cereal are mixtures because both contain two or more kinds of matter that are mixed together physically but not chemically. Because the kinds of matter in a mixture are not chemically combined, it is possible to separate the parts based on their physical properties.

PURPOSE

In this activity, you will observe and analyze the separation of mixtures based on four physical properties of matter—the ability to dissolve in water, the ability to float on water, magnetism, and size.

PROCEDURE

1. Copy the chart in Figure 4-17. Put on safety goggles, a lab apron, and plastic gloves.

2. Spread two or three sheets of paper towels on your work area.

3. Obtain a clear plastic cup and put in one teaspoon of sand and one teaspoon of Epsom salt. Record your observations of the two substances on the chart. With a stirrer, mix the two substances together.

4. Cover one end of a bar magnet with plastic wrap and insert it into the cup with the mixture. Use the magnet to stir the mixture. Take the magnet out and examine it closely. Record your observations.

5. Obtain a cup of water and pour it into the cup with the mixture. Stir the mixture with the stirrer. Record your observations.

6. Line a sieve with filter paper. Place the sieve over the mouth of a beaker. Pour the mixture into the sieve. Record your observations.

7. Dispose of the mixture in a waste beaker. Rinse and dry out the plastic cup, the sieve, and the first beaker.

8. Repeat Steps 2 through 6 using sand, sawdust, and iron filings to make another mixture. Follow your teacher's directions on how to add iron filings to the mixture.

▲ **STEP 6** Pour the mixture into the sieve.

◀ **Figure 4-16** Iron filings, sand, and sawdust mixture

Separating Mixtures				
Substance	Dissolves in Water	Floats in Water	Magnetic	Filtered by Sieve
Epsom salt				
Iron				
Sand				
Sawdust				

▲ **Figure 4-17** Copy this chart and use it to record your observations.

CONCLUSIONS

1. **INFER:** Describe how each substance was able to keep its own physical properties when it was mixed with another substance.

2. **INFER:** How do you know that each combination was not a chemical combination?

3. **ANALYZE:** Design procedures to separate each mixture into its parts.

4-5 What is an ionic bond?

Objective
Describe how atoms form ionic bonds.

Key Terms
valence electron: electron in the outermost energy level of an atom

ion (EYE-uhn)**:** atom with an electrical charge

ionic bond: bond formed between atoms that have gained or lost electrons

Valence Electrons The formation of chemical bonds is a process involving valence electrons. A **valence electron** is an electron in the outermost energy level of an atom. Except for the elements hydrogen and helium, the outermost energy level of an atom can hold a maximum of eight electrons. An atom with eight electrons in its outermost energy level is very stable.

Atoms of all elements have valence electrons. Atoms with fewer than eight valence electrons tend to form bonds with other atoms. Atoms can give electrons, receive electrons, or share electrons with other atoms to reach the stable number of eight valence electrons.

▶ **1 DEFINE:** What are valence electrons?

Neutral Atoms All matter is made up of atoms. Every atom is made up of smaller particles called protons, neutrons, and electrons. A proton has a positive charge. An electron has a negative charge. A neutron has no charge.

In an atom, the number of protons and the number of electrons are the same. Because the charges are balanced, all atoms are neutral.

▶ **2 EXPLAIN:** Why are atoms neutral?

Charged Atoms When forming chemical bonds, the atoms of nonmetals tend to gain electrons while the atoms of metals tend to lose electrons. When the number of electrons in an atom is different from the number of protons, the atom becomes electrically charged. An atom with an electrical charge is called an **ion.**

If a neutral atom gains electrons, it becomes a negative ion. It is a negative ion because there are now more electrons than there are protons. Electrons have a negative charge. If a neutral atom loses electrons, it becomes a positive ion. There are more protons than there are electrons.

▶ **3 COMPARE:** Does a negative ion have more protons or more electrons?

Ionic Bonds In compounds, particles of matter are held together by chemical bonds. A bond that forms when one atom gains one or more electrons from another atom is called an **ionic bond.** The atom that gains electrons becomes a negative ion. The atom that loses electrons becomes a positive ion. The two ions have opposite electrical charges. As a result, they are attracted to each other. This force of attraction holds atoms together in an ionic bond.

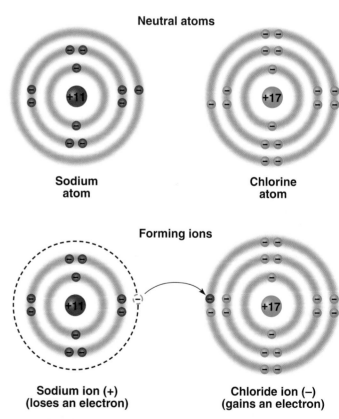

Neutral atoms

Sodium atom   Chlorine atom

Forming ions

Sodium ion (+)
(loses an electron)

Chloride ion (–)
(gains an electron)

▲ **Figure 4-18** Atoms of sodium and chlorine form ionic bonds.

▶ **4 EXPLAIN:** How does an ionic bond form?

Ionic Compounds Compounds whose atoms are held together by ionic bonds are called ionic compounds. Ionic compounds are not made up of molecules. Instead, they are made up of one or more positive ions and one or more negative ions. Because the atoms are held together by ionic bonds, ionic compounds have similar properties. One of these properties is crystal shape. A crystal is a solid that contains atoms arranged in a regular pattern. Many ionic compounds, such as sodium chloride, form crystals. Ionic compounds also have high melting points and they are conductors of electricity when they are melted.

 IDENTIFY: What is a crystal?

✓ CHECKING CONCEPTS

1. Electrons have a _____ electrical charge.
2. When an atom loses electrons, it becomes a _____ ion.
3. An _____ forms when one atom takes an electron from another atom.
4. Particles with opposite electrical charges _____ each other.

5. An ionic compound is not made up of _____.
6. A _____ is a solid that contains atoms arranged in a regular pattern.

THINKING CRITICALLY

7. **INFER:** Could an atom ever lose an electron without another atom gaining the electron? Explain.
8. **ANALYZE:** Why are ionic compounds not made of molecules?

BUILDING SCIENCE SKILLS

Modeling Crystal A crystal is a solid that contains atoms arranged in a regular pattern. The pattern of atoms forms a crystal lattice. The shape of a crystal is determined by its crystal lattice. Table salt, or sodium chloride, is an example of a crystal. Research the type of crystal lattice found in table salt. Draw a diagram of the crystal lattice of sodium chloride and display it to the class. Label the sodium ions and chloride ions in the lattice.

How Do They Know That?

CRYSTALLOGRAPHY

Crystals have been the object of scientific study for hundreds of years. Early mineralogists classified crystals according to observable properties such as shape and color. Around 1800, mineralogists began measuring the angles found on a crystal's surface. The mineralogists thought that the size of a crystal's angles was related to the type of substances that make up the crystal. However, they had no way of looking at the internal structure of a crystal.

 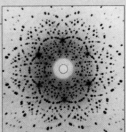

▲ **Figure 4-19** A beryl crystal (left) and an X-ray of beryl (right)

In 1895, X-rays were discovered. Using X-rays, scientists could examine the structure of crystals. They discovered that crystal angles are caused by common structural patterns inside the crystal. As a result of X-ray crystallography, scientists were able to identify six basic crystal systems. The names of these crystal systems are cubic, tetragonal, orthorhombic, monoclinic, hexagonal/trigonal, and triclinic.

Thinking Critically How do you think the names of the crystal systems are related to their shapes? Use a reference to find out.

4-6 What is a covalent bond?

Objective
Describe how atoms combine in covalent bonds.

Key Term
covalent bond: bond formed when atoms share electrons

Outermost Energy Levels In most atoms, the outermost energy level is not completely filled. The outermost energy level does not contain the maximum number of valence electrons that it can hold. In order to complete their outermost energy levels, atoms gain, lose, or share electrons. These electrons come from other atoms that also have incomplete outermost energy levels.

Ionic bonds form when one atom gains one or more electrons from another atom. The result is an ionic compound. Elements can also form compounds when their atoms share electrons to form a molecule. This type of bonding is called a **covalent bond.**

▶ **IDENTIFY:** How can atoms complete their outermost energy levels?

Covalent Compounds Compounds whose atoms share electrons in covalent bonds are called covalent compounds. The shared electrons are in the outermost energy levels of all the atoms in a molecule of the covalent compound.

Water is an example of a covalent compound. A water molecule has covalent bonds between an atom of oxygen and two atoms of hydrogen. The oxygen atom has six electrons in its outermost energy level. It needs two more electrons to completely fill this energy level. A hydrogen atom has one electron in its one and only energy level. This energy level is complete when it has two electrons. So, a hydrogen atom needs only one more electron to fill its outermost energy level. Figure 4-20 shows the covalent bonds in a molecule of water. Notice how two atoms of hydrogen form covalent bonds with one atom of oxygen to form the water molecule.

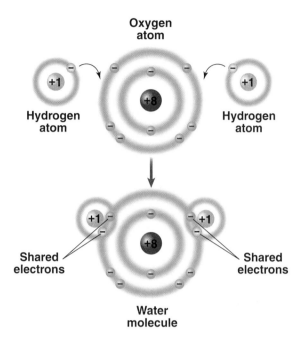

▲ **Figure 4-20** A molecule of water has covalent bonds between the atoms of hydrogen and the atom of oxygen.

▶ **CLASSIFY:** Is water an ionic compound or a covalent compound?

Comparing Ionic and Covalent Compounds Covalent compounds are formed differently from ionic compounds. Atoms joined by a covalent bond do not lose or gain electrons. So, they do not become positively or negatively charged. They do not become ions. The atoms remain neutral. Figure 4-21 lists the main points to know about ionic compounds and covalent compounds.

COMPARING IONIC AND COVALENT COMPOUNDS	
Ionic Compounds	**Covalent Compounds**
Atoms complete their outermost energy levels.	Atoms complete their outermost energy levels.
Electrons are lost and gained.	Electrons are shared.
Atoms form ions.	Atoms remain neutral.

▲ **Figure 4-21** Ionic compounds and covalent compounds act differently.

▶ **COMPARE:** How are covalent compounds different from ionic compounds?

Electron Dot Diagrams Electron dot diagrams include the symbols of the elements in a compound and the arrangement of the valence electrons for each element. These diagrams can be used to show the positive and negative ions in an ionic compound. They can also be used to show a molecule of a covalent compound. Figure 4-22 shows the electron dot diagrams for sodium chloride and water.

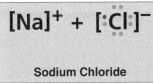

Sodium Chloride   **Water**

 Figure 4-22 Electron dot diagrams for an ionic compound (left) and a covalent compound (right)

4 INFER: What do electron dot diagrams show?

✓ CHECKING CONCEPTS

1. In most atoms, the _____ energy level is not completely filled.

2. In a covalent bond, electrons are _____.

3. Water is an example of a _____ compound.

4. In a covalent compound, the atoms join together to form a _____.

5. In a covalent compound, the atoms remain _____.

6. Diagrams that show the symbol of the elements in a compound and the arrangement of the electrons for each element are called _____.

💡 THINKING CRITICALLY

7. HYPOTHESIZE: A carbon atom has four valence electrons in its outermost energy level. An oxygen atom has six valence electrons. Hypothesize about the type of bonding that will take place between carbon and oxygen.

 Hands-On Activity

MAKING A MOLECULAR MODEL

You will need white and red modeling clay, and toothpicks.

1. Using the red clay, make four round balls that are the same size.

2. Make one round ball of white clay that is the same size as the red balls.

3. Use toothpicks to connect each of the four red balls to the white ball. Space the red balls equally around the white ball. You have just made a model of a methane molecule. A molecule of methane contains four hydrogen atoms joined to one carbon atom.

▲ **STEP 3** Make a model of a methane molecule.

Practicing Your Skills

4. OBSERVE: What element is represented by the red balls?

5. OBSERVE: What element is represented by the white ball?

6. ANALYZE: What type of bond joins the atoms?

7. ANALYZE: Do the atoms in a methane molecule have an electrical charge? Why or why not?

4-7 What is an organic compound?

Objective
Identify some organic compounds.

Key Terms
organic compound: compound containing carbon

organic chemistry: study of organic compounds

structural formula: molecular model that uses straight lines to indicate bonds

polymers: large molecules that are formed by many smaller molecules

Classifying Compounds Scientists classify compounds based on which ones contain the element carbon and which ones do not. The compounds that contain carbon are called **organic compounds.** The compounds that do not usually contain carbon are called inorganic compounds. An example of an organic compound is sugar, which is made up of carbon, hydrogen, and oxygen. An example of an inorganic compound is water. Water is made up of oxygen and hydrogen.

At one time, scientists thought that only living things contained organic compounds. Today, scientists know that some nonliving substances, such as plastics, contain organic compounds. Also, the compounds carbon dioxide and carbon monoxide are classified as inorganic compounds even though they do contain carbon.

▶ **DEFINE:** What is an organic compound?

Organic Chemistry About 95% of all known substances are organic compounds. Because so many of the compounds around us are organic compounds, the study of these substances has been given its own special branch of science called **organic chemistry.**

Scientists studying organic chemistry have learned that a molecule of an organic compound can contain large numbers of atoms. This can happen because a carbon atom has four electrons in its outermost energy level. As a result, a carbon atom can form covalent bonds with up to four other atoms. A carbon atom can form three

different kinds of covalent bonds—a single bond, a double bond, and a triple bond.

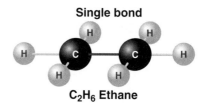

Single bond

In a single bond, a carbon atom shares one pair of electrons with another atom.

C_2H_6 Ethane

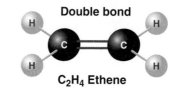

Double bond

In a double bond, two pairs of electrons are shared between atoms.

C_2H_4 Ethene

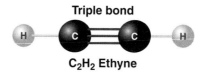

Triple bond

In a triple bond, three pairs of electrons are shared between atoms.

C_2H_2 Ethyne

▲ **Figure 4-23** Three types of covalent bonds allow many different organic compounds to be formed.

▶ **IDENTIFY:** What is organic chemistry?

Structural Formulas When carbon atoms join together, they can form many different atomic structures. The atoms can join in a straight chain or a branched chain, or curve around in a ring. These arrangements of atoms can be shown in a structural formula. A **structural formula** is a molecular model that uses straight lines to show bonds. Structural formulas are frequently used to represent organic compounds. Figure 4-24 shows the structural formulas of some organic compounds.

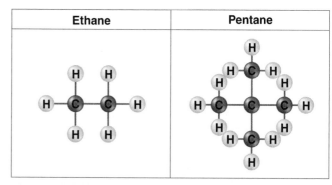

| Ethane | Pentane |

▲ **Figure 4-24** Structural formulas

▶ **IDENTIFY:** What is a structural formula?

Polymers Organic compounds can join together to form very large molecules. These molecules can contain thousands or even millions of atoms. Very large molecules that are formed by many smaller molecules are called **polymers.** The smaller molecules that make up polymers are called monomers.

You may be familiar with some polymers, such as silk, nylon and wool. Many kinds of polymers are used to make materials that we use every day. Some products made from polymers include foam drinking cups, garden hoses, milk containers, and automobile parts.

 LIST: Name some products made from polymers.

 CHECKING CONCEPTS

1. All organic compounds contain the element _____.

2. A carbon atom can form covalent bonds with up to _____ other atoms.

3. In a _____ bond, two pairs of electrons are shared between atoms.

4. The study of organic compounds is called _____.

5. A _____ shows the arrangement of atoms in a molecule of an organic compound.

6. Very large molecules made up of many smaller molecules are called _____.

THINKING CRITICALLY

7. **INFER:** An atom of hydrogen contains one electron in its one energy level. Could a hydrogen atom form a triple bond with another atom? Explain your answer.

8. **EXPLAIN:** Why are there more organic compounds than inorganic compounds?

INTERPRETING VISUALS

Use Figure 4-24 to help you answer the following questions.

9. What is the chemical formula of ethane?

10. What is the chemical formula of pentane?

Science and Technology
ISOMERS

A structural formula can show you that a certain kind of organic compound can have different arrangements. Two or more compounds that have the same chemical makeup but different structures are called **isomers.** For example, Figure 4-25 shows the two structural formulas for the compound butane. Each isomer has four carbon atoms and ten hydrogen atoms in each of its molecules. However, the atoms of each isomer are arranged differently. One isomer is a straight chain and the other isomer is a branched chain. Because each molecule has a different arrangement, each compound has different physical and chemical properties.

Organic compounds that have a large number of carbon atoms may have many isomers. In general, as the number of carbon atoms increases, the number of isomers will also increase.

Thinking Critically Why do you think the number of isomers increases when the number of carbon atoms increases?

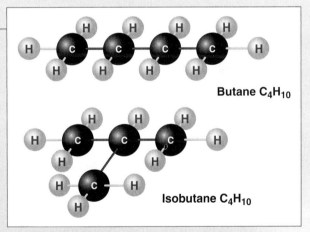

Butane C_4H_{10}

Isobutane C_4H_{10}

▲ **Figure 4-25** Butane (top) and isobutane (bottom) are isomers.

4-8 What organic compounds are needed by living things?

Objective
Identify organic compounds needed by living things.

Key Terms
carbohydrates (kahr-boh-HY-drayts)**:** sugars and starches

lipids: fats and oils

proteins: compounds used to build and repair body tissues

amino acids: building blocks of proteins

nucleic acids: compounds made up of carbon, oxygen, hydrogen, nitrogen, and phosphorus

▲ **Figure 4-26** Sources of lipids

Needs of Living Things All living things need certain organic compounds to stay alive. An organism gets the organic compounds it needs from its food. Most foods are made up of carbohydrates, lipids, and proteins.

▶ 1 **IDENTIFY:** How do organisms obtain the organic compounds they need?

Carbohydrates The organic compounds made up of carbon, hydrogen, and oxygen are called carbohydrates. Sugars and starches are both **carbohydrates**. These organic compounds are the body's main source of energy. Foods such as cereals, grains, pasta, vegetables, and fruits are good sources of carbohydrates.

▶ 2 **EXPLAIN:** Why do all living things need carbohydrates?

Lipids The organic compounds that are made up mostly of carbon and hydrogen are called lipids. Fats and oils are **lipids**. These compounds are another energy source for the body. Lipids can be stored in the body for use at a later time. For this reason, lipids are often called the body's stored energy supply. Foods such as butter, meat, cheese, and nuts are good sources of lipids.

Cholesterol is a kind of lipid. Animal fat contains cholesterol. Eating too many foods high in certain kinds of cholesterol can be harmful to the body. Excess amounts of cholesterol may form fatty deposits on the walls of blood vessels. These fatty deposits can interfere with the flow of blood through the body.

▶ 3 **DESCRIBE:** Why do living things need lipids?

Proteins Organic compounds that are used to build and repair the body are called **proteins**. Proteins are made up of substances called **amino acids**. Amino acids contain carbon, hydrogen, oxygen, and nitrogen. Amino acids join together in long chains to form proteins. For this reason, amino acids are called the building blocks of proteins. Meat, milk, fish, eggs, and beans are good sources of protein. Foods such as fish and soybeans provide the body with most of the amino acids it needs.

▲ **Figure 4-27** Sources of amino acids and proteins

▶ 4 **RELATE:** What is the relationship between amino acids and proteins?

Nucleic Acids Other organic compounds that your body needs are called nucleic acids. **Nucleic acids** are made up of carbon, oxygen, hydrogen, nitrogen, and phosphorus. There are two types of nucleic acids, deoxyribonucleic acid (DNA) and ribonucleic acid (RNA). These organic compounds are made up of very large molecules. Each molecule is a type of polymer made up of chains of smaller molecules joined together. You have probably heard of DNA. It contains the information about the characteristics that you have inherited and it also controls the activities of the cells in your body.

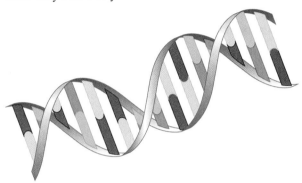

▲ **Figure 4-28** Section of a DNA molecule

5 ▶ DESCRIBE: What elements are nucleic acids made up of?

✓ CHECKING CONCEPTS

1. An organism gets the organic compounds it needs from its _____.
2. Organic compounds made up of carbon, hydrogen, and oxygen are called _____.
3. Sugars and starches are _____.
4. Fats and oils are _____.
5. Organic compounds used to build and repair body parts are called _____.
6. The organic compounds that control the activities in body cells are called _____.

THINKING CRITICALLY

7. **INFER:** Why do many long-distance runners eat a meal of pasta before running a race?

BUILDING SCIENCE SKILLS

Organizing Information Make a table with the following headings: *Carbohydrates*, *Lipids*, and *Proteins*. Under each heading, identify five types of foods that you enjoy eating which contain that type of organic compound.

Real-Life Science

FOOD PYRAMID

To keep your body healthy you should eat a balanced diet. One way to get a balanced diet is to follow the Food Guide Pyramid.

The pyramid shows the six food groups that provide important organic compounds. It also tells how much food you should eat from each group every day. The bottom row of the pyramid is the bread, cereal, rice, and pasta group. These foods contain carbohydrates. The second row of the pyramid contains the vegetable group and the fruit group. The foods in these groups contain carbohydrates and other substances your body needs. The third level contains the milk, yogurt, and cheese group and the meat, poultry, fish, dry beans, eggs, and nuts group. These two groups contain proteins. The group at the top of the pyramid is the fats, oils, and sweets group. Foods from this group should be eaten in small amounts.

Thinking Critically How does the food pyramid tell you how much food you should eat from each group?

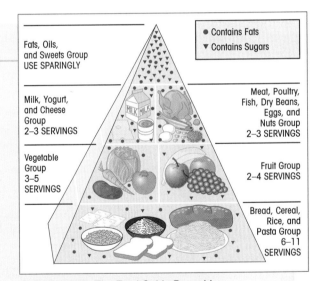

▲ **Figure 4-29** The Food Guide Pyramid

THE Big IDEA

What organisms produce poisonous compounds?

Your bones and your organs are very different in chemical structure. Yet, they are all made up of molecules. It takes thousands of different molecules to make up one cell and even more to make up a whole human. Many molecules in living things are complex. We can learn a lot by studying the variety of molecules in Earth's living things.

The cells in all organisms can make different kinds of molecules. Some of these molecules make compounds that help organisms to grow, to fight germs, and to make new cells when old cells die. Some organisms can even make molecules that form poisonous substances.

Poisons from living things are called toxins. Animals and plants that produce toxins are very successful at defending themselves against predators. These organisms can also pass on their ability to make the toxic substances to future generations. Over millions of years, some organisms have evolved to produce very strong toxins.

Some organisms that can produce toxins include the strychnos (STRIHK-nohs) vine, the cinchona (sihn-KOH-nuh) plant, many kinds of snakes, and some tropical frogs.

Look at the photographs of the organisms that appear on these two pages. Read about the poisons that they produce. Find out how some of their poisons can be used in medicines that help treat certain diseases. Then, follow the directions in the Science Log. Go on your own adventure to find other organisms that produce special molecules. ✦

Cinchona Plant

The cinchona plant is grown in countries in South America, India, and parts of Africa. The bark of this poisonous tree is used to make a medicine for the fever caused by the disease malaria. Taking too much of the medicine may, however, lead to coma and death.

Poison Dart Frog

The poison dart frog is a colorful rain-forest frog. It produces strong toxins in its skin. These toxins can cause paralysis and eventually death if absorbed into the bloodstream of other animals. The frogs' bright color warns predators not to eat it.

Science Log

Sometimes biochemists travel the world looking for useful molecules in exotic organisms. In your science log, plan a research trip. In what part of the world would you look for useful molecules in plants and animals? What are some uses of these molecules? Start your search at www.conceptsandchallenges.com.

WRITING ACTIVITY

Strychnos Vine

The strychnos vine makes toxic molecules in its bark. Native peoples of South America use it to make a poison used in hunting called curari. A medicine that helps treat rabies has been made from this poison.

Saw Scaled Viper

The saw scaled viper is usually found in very dry desert regions. It makes a highly poisonous toxin. A bite from this snake causes its victim to bleed to death. Medical researchers have studied this toxin to help them make a drug that prevents blood clots in patients at risk for heart attacks.

Chapter 4 Challenges

Chapter Summary

Lesson 4-1

- The three types of matter are **elements**, **compounds**, and **mixtures**.

Lesson 4-2

- A **compound** is a substance made up of two or more elements that are chemically combined.
- Compounds are formed as a result of a chemical change.

Lesson 4-3

- A **mixture** contains two or more substances that have been physically combined.
- The substances in a mixture keep their original properties.

Lesson 4-4

- Mixtures differ from compounds in several ways.

Lesson 4-5

- When an atom gains or loses electrons, it becomes an **ion**.
- An **ionic bond** forms between atoms that gain or lose electrons.

Lesson 4-6

- A **covalent bond** forms when atoms share electrons.

Lesson 4-7

- **Organic compounds** contain the element carbon and can form many different structures.

Lesson 4-8

- Organic compounds needed by living things include **carbohydrates**, **lipids**, **proteins**, and **nucleic acids**.

Key Term Challenges

amino acids (p. 96)
carbohydrates (p. 96)
chemical bond (p. 82)
compound (p. 80)
covalent bond (p. 92)
element (p. 80)
ion (p. 90)
ionic bond (p. 90)
lipids (p. 96)
mixture (p. 80)
molecule (p. 82)
nucleic acids (p. 96)
organic chemistry (p. 94)
organic compound (p. 94)
polymer (p. 94)
proteins (p. 96)
structural formula (p. 94)
substance (p. 80)
valence electron (p. 90)

MATCHING Write the Key Term from above that best matches each description.

1. any element or compound

2. study of organic compounds

3. compounds containing carbon

4. bond formed when atoms share electrons

5. fats and oils

6. sugars and starches

FILL IN Write the Key Term from above that best completes each statement.

7. Salt water is an example of a _____.

8. An atom with an electrical charge is called an _____.

9. The force of attraction that holds atoms together is a _____.

10. Very large molecules that are made of a chain of many smaller molecules are called _____.

Content Challenges TEST PREP

MULTIPLE CHOICE **Write the letter of the term or phrase that best completes each statement.**

1. The compound formed when hydrogen and oxygen combine chemically is
   a. salt.
   b. water.
   c. sugar.
   d. sand.

2. Compounds are formed as a result of
   a. evaporation.
   b. filtration.
   c. a physical change.
   d. a chemical change.

3. A molecule is the smallest part of
   a. a crystal.
   b. a substance.
   c. an atom.
   d. compounds.

4. A salt and water mixture can be separated by
   a. hand.
   b. filtering.
   c. melting.
   d. evaporating.

5. The compound iron sulfide can be formed by
   a. heating.
   b. filtering.
   c. evaporating.
   d. mixing.

6. A molecular model of an organic compound is called a
   a. molecular formula.
   b. compound structure.
   c. structural formula.
   d. compound formula.

7. A covalent bond is formed when atoms
   a. trade electrons.
   b. gain electrons.
   c. lose electrons.
   d. share electrons.

8. In an ionic bond, two atoms form
   a. ions.
   b. protons.
   c. neutrons.
   d. electrons.

9. All organic compounds contain
   a. hydrogen.
   b. oxygen.
   c. nitrogen.
   d. carbon.

10. The building blocks of protein are
    a. carbohydrates.
    b. molecules.
    c. ions.
    d. amino acids.

TRUE/FALSE **Write *true* if the statement is true. If the statement is false, change the underlined term to make the statement true.**

11. The three main groups of <u>substances</u> are elements, compounds, and mixtures.

12. The substances in a mixture have not been <u>chemically</u> combined.

13. You can <u>physically</u> separate a mixture of sand and water.

14. A <u>compound</u> is made up of two or more elements.

15. An <u>ionic</u> bond is formed between two atoms that have gained or lost electrons.

16. <u>Nucleic acids</u> control the activities of a cell.

Concept Challenges TEST PREP

WRITTEN RESPONSE Answer each of the following questions in complete sentences.

1. **DESCRIBE:** Describe a method of separating each of the following mixtures:
   a. sand and sugar
   b. sugar and water
   c. sawdust and iron filings
   d. nickels and dimes

2. **COMPARE:** How are ionic and covalent compounds the same? How are they different?

3. **EXPLAIN:** How are the properties of table salt different from the properties of the elements that make it up?

4. **PREDICT:** What might happen if you did not get enough carbohydrates in your diet? Explain your answer.

5. **ANALYZE:** Why can carbon form so many different kinds of compounds?

INTERPRETING A DIAGRAM Use Figure 4-30 to answer the following questions.

6. What kind of compound is formed in Diagram B?

7. How many electrons are there in the outermost energy level of a neutral oxygen atom?

8. How many protons are there in a neutral oxygen atom? In a neutral hydrogen atom?

9. How many electrons does an atom of oxygen need in order to complete its outermost energy level?

10. What kind of bonds are being formed?

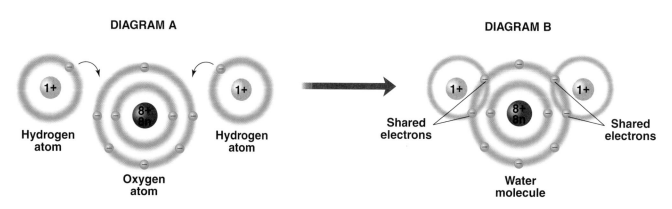

▲ **Figure 4-30** Forming a water molecule

Chapter 5 Solutions

▲ **Figure 5-1** A surfer is riding the "saltwater solution."

Surfers travel the world looking for the "perfect wave." In our culture, the ocean is important to us for many things. It supplies us with entertainment, food, travel, and shipping. More than three-fourths of Earth is covered by water. About 97% of that is ocean. Ocean water is the largest solution we know of. It contains many salts and minerals.

▶What makes the ocean's water so important to us?

Contents

5-1 What is a solution?

INVESTIGATE

Identifying a Solution
HANDS-ON ACTIVITY

1. Put 50 mL of water into a clear plastic cup. Add 1 tsp of pepper and stir.

2. Put the same amount of water in a second cup, and add 1 tsp of salt. Stir.

3. Compare the two mixtures.

THINK ABOUT IT: What differences do you observe? Can you infer which mixture is a solution? On what do you base your inference?

STEP 1

Objective
Describe the characteristics of a solution.

Key Terms
dissolve (dih-ZAHLV)**:** go into solution

solution: mixture in which the particles of one substance are evenly mixed with the particles of another substance

Salt and Water What would happen if you added some sand to a test tube of water? The sand would settle to the bottom of the test tube. Suppose you then added some salt to another test tube of water. The salt seems to disappear in the water. The salt is still in the water, but you cannot see it. The salt has dissolved in the water. When a substance **dissolves,** it goes into solution. The sand did not dissolve in the water.

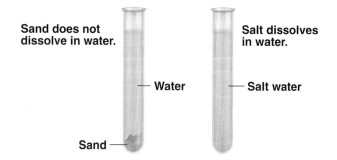

Sand does not dissolve in water.

— Water

Salt dissolves in water.

— Salt water

Sand —

▲ **Figure 5-2** One test tube holds a solution. The other does not.

 EXPLAIN: Why does salt seem to disappear in water?

Solutions A mixture of salt and water is an example of a solution. A **solution** is a mixture in which the particles (molecules or ions) of one substance are evenly mixed with the particles of another substance. In a saltwater solution, sodium ions and chlorine ions are evenly mixed with molecules of water.

2 **DEFINE:** What is a solution?

Types of Solutions Liquid solutions are formed when solids, liquids, or gases dissolve in liquids. Salt water is a liquid solution. A liquid solution may also be formed when a gas dissolves in a liquid. Club soda is a solution of the gas carbon dioxide dissolved in water. Liquids may dissolve in other liquids.

Solutions can also be formed when different substances dissolve in solids and gases. Figure 5-3 shows some examples of different kinds of solutions.

TYPES OF SOLUTIONS		
Substance	**Dissolved in**	**Examples**
Liquid	Liquid	Antifreeze (ethylene glycol) in water
	Gas	Water droplets in air (fog)
	Solid	Ether in rubber
Gas	Liquid	Club soda (CO_2 in water)
	Gas	Air (O_2 and other gases in N_2)
	Solid	Hydrogen in palladium
Solid	Liquid	Salt in water (ocean)
	Gas	Iodine vapor in air
	Solid	Brass (zinc in copper)

▲ **Figure 5-3**

 LIST: What are the different types of solutions?

Other Solutions Tap water, the water you use every day, is not pure water. It is a solution. Most tap water contains dissolved compounds of iron and compounds of calcium. Tap water may also contain dissolved chemicals, such as chlorine, that have been added to make the water safe to drink. Pure air is a solution of gases, mainly nitrogen and oxygen, evenly mixed together.

 ANALYZE: Why is pure air called a solution?

✓ CHECKING CONCEPTS

1. Solutions are formed when substances _____ in other substances.

2. Salt water is a solution formed when a _____ dissolves in a liquid.

3. A mixture in which one substance is evenly mixed with another substance is called a _____.

4. Club soda is an example of a solution formed when a _____ dissolves in a liquid.

5. Pure air is a solution of gases, such as _____ and _____.

THINKING CRITICALLY

6. **CLASSIFY:** Which of the following mixtures are solutions?
   - **a.** sugar and water
   - **b.** brass
   - **c.** club soda
   - **d.** flour and salt
   - **e.** sea water
   - **f.** salt and pepper
   - **g.** sand and water
   - **h.** air

7. **ANALYZE:** For each of the mixtures you classified as solutions in question 6, identify the type of solution formed.

Web InfoSearch

Hard Water Because tap water is not pure water, it does not freeze at exactly 0°C. Instead, it freezes at a lower temperature. Tap water containing high concentrations of dissolved salts of calcium, iron, and magnesium is called hard water. This is because the salts make it hard for soap to form a lather with the water.

SEARCH: Find out how these solutes are added to your tap water. Start your search at www.conceptsandchallenges.com. Some key search words are **tap water**, **hard water**, and **water solutes**.

People in Science
ANALYTICAL CHEMIST

Do you enjoy studying science and mathematics? Can you make careful, precise measurements? Are you determined to find the answer to a problem? If so, you may enjoy a career as an analytical chemist. Analytical chemists analyze the chemical composition of substances. They perform experiments to identify characteristics of the substances and to find out what will happen when different substances are combined.

▲ **Figure 5-4** Dr. Sherman K. W. Fung

Most analytical chemists work in laboratories. Dr. Sherman K. W. Fung is such a chemist. He founded and directed the Bio-Sciences Division of SGS Hong Kong Limited, a testing, inspection, and verification organization. Currently, he serves as chief operating officer of the Institute of Chinese Medicine in Hong Kong, China.

To become an analytical chemist, you need a college degree in chemistry. Dr. Fung studied at the University of London and Oxford University.

Thinking Critically Why is it important to be precise and detailed in this line of work?

5-2 What are the parts of a solution?

Objective

Identify the parts of a solution.

Key Terms

solute (SAHL-yoot): substance that is dissolved in a solvent

solvent: substance in which a solute dissolves

soluble (SAHL-yoo-buhl): able to dissolve

solubility: maximum amount of a substance that will dissolve in a given quantity of a solvent at a given temperature

insoluble (in-SAHL-yoo-buhl): not able to dissolve

Parts of a Solution All solutions are made when one substance dissolves in another substance. A solution of salt and water forms when salt dissolves in water. The part of a solution that dissolves is called the **solute.** Salt is the solute in a solution of salt and water. The part of the solution in which a solute dissolves is called the **solvent.** This substance is usually present in the greater amount, so water is the solvent in a saltwater solution. In pure air, nitrogen is present in the greatest amount of three gases; it is the solvent. Oxygen and argon are the solutes.

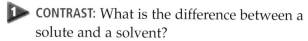 **CONTRAST:** What is the difference between a solute and a solvent?

Soluble Substances In many solutions, the solute becomes invisible. For example, when sugar dissolves in water, the solution looks like plain water. When some substances dissolve, they produce a colored solution. Look at Figure 5-5 at the top of the next column. The picture on the left shows a crystal of potassium permanganate just after it has been placed in a test tube containing water. The picture on the right shows the same test tube a few minutes later. The crystal has begun to dissolve. If the test tube is allowed to sit long enough, or if the mixture is stirred, the entire solution will be a uniform pink color.

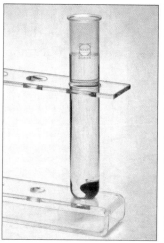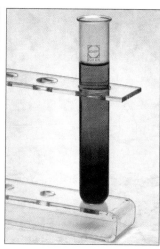

▲ **Figure 5-5** Potassium permanganate dissolves slowly in water. After a few minutes, the solution becomes pink.

Some substances are more **soluble,** able to dissolve, than other substances. The **solubility** of a substance tells you how much of that substance will dissolve in 100 g of solvent at a given temperature. For example, about 38 g of sodium chloride will dissolve in 100 g of water at 20°C. If you add more than 38 g of sodium chloride to this solution, the excess will not dissolve. It will sink to the bottom of the solution.

2 PREDICT: What will happen when a substance that is soluble in water is mixed with water?

Insoluble Substances Many substances do not dissolve in water. A granite statue does not dissolve in rainwater. Sand does not dissolve in ocean water. A drinking glass does not dissolve when you pour water into it. All of these materials are said to be **insoluble,** or not able to dissolve, in water. A substance that will not dissolve in a given solvent, such as water, is said to be insoluble in that solvent.

You may have heard the saying "water and oil don't mix." This saying means that oil is not soluble in water. If you add oil to a glass of water, the oil will float in a separate layer on top of the water. Even if you stir or shake the mixture, no dissolving will take place. Instead, you will get a mixture like the one shown in Figure 5-6 on the next page. In a short time, this mixture will again separate into its two layers.

▲ Figure 5-6 Oil droplets do not dissolve in water.

A substance may dissolve in one solvent but not in another solvent. For example, sugar will dissolve in water but will not dissolve in vegetable oil. So, sugar can be described as being soluble in water and insoluble in vegetable oil. The chemical makeup of a solvent determines whether another substance is soluble or insoluble in that solvent.

 ANALYZE: How can a substance be both soluble and insoluble?

✓ CHECKING CONCEPTS

1. Salt is the _____ in a saltwater solution.
2. In air, _____ is the solvent.
3. The substance in which a solute dissolves is called a _____.
4. Sugar is _____ in water.
5. In a solution of sugar and water, water is the _____.

💡 THINKING CRITICALLY

6. CLASSIFY: Instant coffee is a solution formed from powdered coffee and hot water. Identify the solute and the solvent in this solution.

7. INFER: Is wood soluble in water? How do you know?

DESIGNING AN EXPERIMENT

Design an experiment to solve the following problem. Include a hypothesis, variables, a procedure, and a type of data to study.

PROBLEM: Identify the solute and solvent in iced tea.

 Integrating Earth Science

TOPIC: chemical weathering

AN ACIDIC SOLUTION

Weathering is the breaking down of rocks and minerals by natural forces, such as wind and water. In mechanical weathering, rocks are broken down by the action of wind, water, or ice. In chemical weathering, substances in water cause substances in the rock to dissolve. This action weakens the structure of the rock. The rock is then more easily broken apart by mechanical weathering.

A common type of chemical weathering takes place when carbon dioxide from the air dissolves in rainwater. A solution called carbonic acid forms. When this weak acid seeps into rocks, it

▲ Figure 5-7 Carbonic acid has dissolved the features of this limestone face.

dissolves the limestone in the rocks. The dissolved limestone is carried away by the rainwater. As a result, cracks are left in the rocks. Over time, as the rocks are struck by wind or moving water, they will easily crumble.

Thinking Critically What is the difference between chemical and mechanical weathering?

5-3 Why is water a good solvent?

Objective

Explain why water is sometimes called the universal solvent.

Key Term

polar molecule: molecule in which one end has a positive charge and the other end has a negative charge

Water Molecules Water molecules are polar. A **polar molecule** is a molecule in which one end has a positive charge and the other end has a negative charge. A water molecule is made up of two atoms of hydrogen joined to one atom of oxygen. The hydrogen end of a water molecule has a positive charge. The oxygen end of a water molecule has a negative charge.

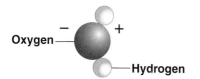

◀ **Figure 5-8** The two ends of a water molecule carry opposite charges.

Water is sometimes called the universal solvent. This is because many types of substances dissolve in water. The electrical charges associated with the polar molecules of water help to dissolve different kinds of substances.

1 EXPLAIN: Why is a water molecule called a polar molecule?

Molecular Solutions The charged ends of a water molecule help separate particles of a solute and spread them throughout the water. Figure 5-9 shows what happens when you place a sugar cube in a glass of water. The ends of the polar water molecules attract the molecules in the sugar cube. Each sugar molecule is pulled to a water molecule. As the sugar dissolves, sugar molecules are evenly mixed throughout the water. This is a molecular solution.

2 DESCRIBE: What happens to the sugar molecules when sugar is placed in water?

Force of Attraction Molecular solutions form when the force of attraction between the solute molecules and the solvent molecules is greater than the forces of attraction holding the molecules of the solute together. A sugar crystal gets its shape from the force of attraction between sugar molecules. The sugar molecules will break away from the sugar crystal only if they are pulled by a greater force of attraction. This is also true of other types of solutes.

3 PREDICT: What will happen if the force of attraction holding solute particles together is greater than the force of attraction between solute and solvent?

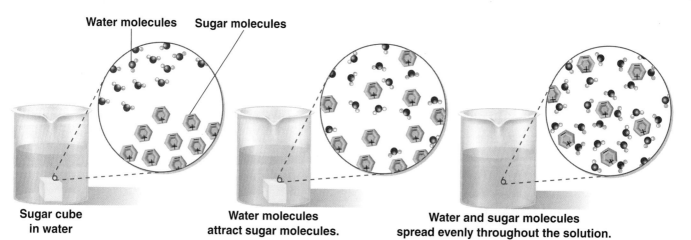

Water molecules   Sugar molecules

Sugar cube in water

Water molecules attract sugar molecules.

Water and sugar molecules spread evenly throughout the solution.

▲ **Figure 5-9** Sugar dissolves in water to form a molecular solution.

Ionic Solutions Ionic compounds are made up of charged particles—positive ions and negative ions. These particles are held together by the force of attraction created by their opposite charges.

When an ionic compound such as sodium chloride—table salt—is added to water, these ions are attracted by the charged ends of the polar molecules of water. In time, the water molecules surround the ions and separate them, as shown in Figure 5-9. The salt dissolves completely, forming an ionic solution.

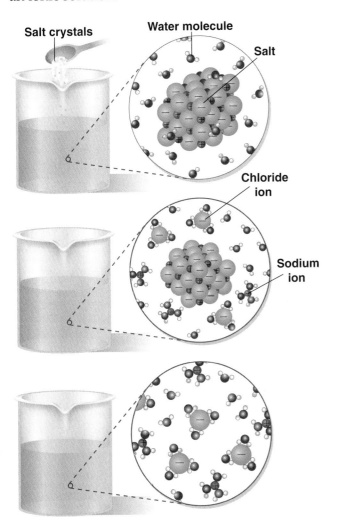

Salt crystals
Water molecule
Salt
Chloride ion
Sodium ion

▲ **Figure 5-10** Salt water is an ionic solution.

▶ **COMPARE:** How are molecular solutions similar to ionic solutions? How are they different?

✓ CHECKING CONCEPTS

1. Water is a _____ molecule.
2. Water is sometimes called the _____ solvent.
3. The hydrogen end of a water molecule has a _____ electrical charge.
4. The force of attraction between water molecules and sugar molecules is _____ than the force of attraction between the sugar molecules.
5. Solutions form when the force of attraction between the solute and the solvent is greater than the force of attraction between the particles of the _____.

💡 THINKING CRITICALLY

6. **INFER:** A substance put in a glass of water does not dissolve. What does this tell you about the force of attraction between the particles of this substance?
7. **HYPOTHESIZE:** Will a teaspoon of water dissolve in a glass of water? Explain. (Hint: Review the definitions of *dissolve* and *solution* from Lesson 5-1.)

Web InfoSearch

Water Purification Chemist Drinking water has to be treated before it reaches your home. A water purification process begins after the water is analyzed. Various tests are performed on the water to find out what chemicals it contains. Based on the results of the tests, chemicals that should be removed from or added to the water to make it suitable for drinking are identified. Most of this work is done in the laboratories of purification plants.

SEARCH: Use the Internet to find out more about water purification chemists. Then create a poster. Start your search at www.conceptsandchallenges.com. Some key search words are **water purification, chemist,** and **purification chemistry.**

5-4 How can you change the rate at which substances dissolve?

Objective
Describe four ways to speed up the rate of dissolving.

Stirring Solutions form when a solute dissolves in a solvent. The rate at which a solid solute dissolves can be changed. Certain factors can speed up the rate at which a solute dissolves. Stirring a solution will make the solute dissolve faster. If you put a cube of sugar into a glass of water, it will eventually dissolve. However, stirring the water will cause the sugar to dissolve faster. Stirring the water causes the sugar molecules to leave the crystals more rapidly.

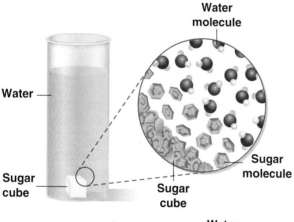

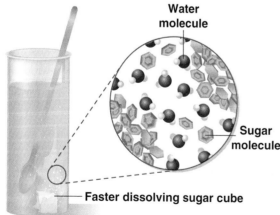

▲ **Figure 5-11** Stirring (bottom) causes sugar to dissolve faster.

▶ **INFER:** Why does stirring make a sugar cube dissolve faster in water?

Temperature The temperature of a liquid solvent affects the rate at which a solid solute dissolves. A cube of sugar dissolves faster in hot water than in an equal amount of cold water. Heat increases the motion of water molecules. This increased energy helps to separate sugar molecules more quickly. As the temperature of a liquid solvent increases, the rate at which a solid solute dissolves also increases.

Some gases, such as oxygen and carbon dioxide, are soluble in water. Increasing the temperature of a liquid solvent has the opposite effect on gaseous solutes than it does on solid solutes. As the temperature of the solvent increases, the dissolving rate of a gaseous solute decreases.

▶ **2 RELATE:** What is the relationship between the temperature of a liquid solvent and the rate at which a solid dissolves in it?

Surface Area The size of the particles of a solid solute also affects the rate at which it dissolves. The smaller the size of the solute particles, the faster the solute dissolves. A crushed sugar cube dissolves faster in water than does a solid sugar cube placed in an equal amount of water at the same temperature. As the size of the solute particles decreases, the rate at which the solute dissolves increases.

▶ **3 PREDICT:** Which would dissolve faster in the same amount of water at the same temperature, a sugar cube or powdered sugar?

Pressure The solubility of most gases is affected by pressure. When pressure is increased, more gas can dissolve. For example, when you open a bottle or can containing a carbonated soft drink, you hear the gas escaping. This is because carbon dioxide is added under high pressure. However, pressure has little effect on the dissolving of solids or liquids.

▶ **4 HYPOTHESIZE:** Why do you think more gas can dissolve when pressure is increased?

Types of Solvents You have learned that water molecules are polar. Water, then, is a polar solvent. Polar solvents such as water will dissolve compounds made up of polar molecules and compounds that separate into ions. However, polar solvents will not dissolve compounds made up of nonpolar molecules, such as oils and fats. These substances will, however, dissolve in nonpolar solvents, such as benzene. A good way to remember this "rule" is "like dissolves like."

 RELATE: What type of compounds will water dissolve?

✓ CHECKING CONCEPTS

1. Stirring a solvent _____ the rate at which a solute dissolves in it.
2. Sugar dissolves more slowly in _____ water than in hot water.
3. The smaller the size of the solute particles, the _____ the rate of dissolving.
4. As the _____ of a solvent increases, the rate at which a solid solute dissolves also increases.

THINKING CRITICALLY

5. **INFER:** Why are most types of instant coffee made in powdered form?
6. **ANALYZE:** Explain how each of the following will make a solid solute dissolve faster.
   a. Grind the solute into small pieces.
   b. Place the solvent in a blender.
   c. Heat the solvent.

DESIGNING AN EXPERIMENT

Design an experiment to solve the following problem. Include a hypothesis, variables, a procedure, and a type of data to study.

PROBLEM: How does changing each of these factors affect the rate at which 5 g of sugar will dissolve in 100 mL of water?

a. stirring
b. temperature
c. surface area

 ## Hands-On Activity

CHANGING THE RATE AT WHICH A SUBSTANCE DISSOLVES

You will need four beakers, a graduated cylinder, water, a spoon, and four sugar cubes.

1. Put 100 mL of water in each beaker.
2. Place one sugar cube in each of the first two beakers. Stir the water in the first beaker with a spoon. Leave the second beaker untouched. Compare the results.
3. Use a spoon to crush a sugar cube. Carefully drop the crushed sugar into the third beaker. Place one sugar cube in the fourth beaker. Stir both mixtures and compare the results.

▲ **STEP 2** See what happens to the sugar cube when the water is stirred.

Practicing Your Skills

4. **OBSERVE:** What effect did stirring have on the dissolving rate of the sugar cube?
5. **OBSERVE:** What effect did crushing the sugar cube have on the rate of dissolving?
6. **HYPOTHESIZE:** How could you find the fastest way to dissolve a sugar cube in 100 mL of water?

5-5 What is the concentration of a solution?

INVESTIGATE

Observing Concentrations
HANDS-ON ACTIVITY

1. Working with a partner, add 100 mL of water to each of two clear plastic glasses.
2. Have one partner face away from the work area. The other partner adds 1/2 tsp of copper sulfate to the water in one glass and 1 tsp of copper sulfate to the water in the other glass and stirs both mixtures.
3. Have the first partner turn and study the two solutions. Ask this student to choose which mixture contains the greater amount of solute.

THINK ABOUT IT: How did the two mixtures differ in appearance? How did this difference help to indicate which solution contained more solute?

STEP 3

Objective

Differentiate between saturated and unsaturated solutions.

Key Terms

dilute solution: solution containing a small amount of solute compared with the amount of solvent present

concentrated solution: solution containing a large amount of solute compared with the amount of solvent present

unsaturated solution: solution containing less solute than it can hold at a given temperature

saturated solution: solution containing all the solute it can hold at a given temperature

supersaturated solution: solution containing more solute than it can normally hold at a given temperature

Dilute and Concentrated Solutions The terms *dilute* and *concentrated* are used to describe the relative amounts of solute and solvent present in a solution. Figure 5-12 shows the appearance of three different concentrations of copper sulfate in 100 mL of water at the same temperature.

As the illustration shows, a **dilute solution** is one containing a small amount of solute compared with the amount of solvent present. Dilute solutions are weak. A **concentrated solution** is one containing a large amount of solute compared with the amount of solvent present. Concentrated solutions are strong.

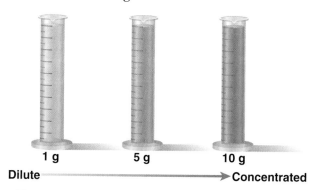

▲ **Figure 5-12** Different concentrations of copper sulfate

1 ▶ **COMPARE:** What is the difference between a dilute solution and a concentrated solution?

Unsaturated Solutions If you were to add 1 g of the compound copper sulfate to 100 mL of water at 20°C, the copper sulfate would quickly dissolve. In fact, quite a bit more copper sulfate could dissolve in that much water at that temperature. This copper sulfate solution is unsaturated. An **unsaturated solution** contains less dissolved solute than it can hold at a given temperature.

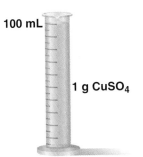

100 mL

1 g CuSO$_4$

◀ **Figure 5-13**
Unsaturated solution
of copper sulfate

2 ▶ **ANALYZE:** When is a solution unsaturated?

Saturated Solutions There is a limit to the amount of solute a given amount of solvent can hold at a specific temperature. If you continued to add copper sulfate to the solution described above, the solution would become saturated. A **saturated solution** contains all of the solute it can hold at a given temperature. If you added more copper sulfate to the saturated solution, it would not dissolve. It would settle out of the solution.

100 mL

20 g CuSO$_4$

◀ **Figure 5-14** Saturated
solution of copper sulfate

3 ▶ **HYPOTHESIZE:** If you were preparing a solution, how could you tell when it became saturated?

Supersaturated Solutions The temperature of a solvent determines the amount of solute it can dissolve. As the temperature of a solvent increases, so does the amount of a given solute it can hold. For example, 100 mL of water at 20°C can hold about 14 g of copper sulfate. The same amount of water at 80°C can hold about five times as much copper sulfate.

Suppose you have a saturated solution of copper sulfate at 50°C. The solution contains as much solute as it can hold at that temperature. What will happen if the solution is allowed to cool? At the lower temperature, the solution will be holding *more* solute than it could normally hold at that temperature. Such a solution is said to be **supersaturated**.

4 ▶ **INFER:** What happens to a solution that enables it to hold more solute than it normally would?

1. A _____ solution contains a small amount of dissolved solute.

2. A _____ solution contains a large amount of dissolved solute.

3. An unsaturated solution contains less _____ than it can hold at a given temperature.

4. A solution that contains all the solute it can hold at a given temperature is called a _____ solution.

5. When saturated solutions are _____, they usually become unsaturated.

THINKING CRITICALLY

6. **HYPOTHESIZE:** Is a can of frozen juice a concentrated or a dilute solution? Explain.

7. **PREDICT:** Suppose the directions on a can of frozen juice state that it should be mixed with three cans of water. What type of solution would you make if you added five cans of water? Explain.

INTERPRETING VISUALS

The graph in Figure 5-15 shows the solubility of ammonia, NH$_3$, and potassium chloride, KCl, at different temperatures. Use the graph to answer the questions.

8. **ANALYZE:** How much more KCl will dissolve in 100mL of water at 100°C than at 0°C?

9. **INFER:** Is NH$_3$ a gas or a solid? How do you know?

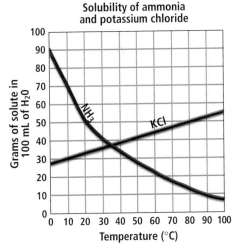

Solubility of ammonia
and potassium chloride

NH$_3$

KCl

▲ **Figure 5-15** Solubility graph

5-6 How do solutes affect freezing point?

Objective

Describe how the presence of a solute affects the freezing point of a liquid solvent.

Key Terms

freezing point: temperature at which a liquid changes to a solid

freezing point depression: decrease in the freezing point of a liquid solvent because of the addition of a solute

Freezing Point of Water The temperature at which a liquid changes to a solid is called its **freezing point.** The freezing point of pure water is 0°C. When pure liquid water reaches this temperature, it begins changing to solid ice. When water freezes, its molecules become arranged in a crystal pattern called a lattice.

Salt water does not freeze at 0°C. The particles of salt dissolved in the water interfere with the change from a liquid to a solid. Because salt water contains dissolved salt and other minerals, its freezing point is lower than that of pure water.

Fresh water	Salt water

Ice	Liquid

▲ **Figure 5-16** Sodium and chloride ions in salt water lower the freezing point of the water. Crystals cannot form unless the temperature is below 0°C.

 DESCRIBE: What happens to liquid water at its freezing point?

Freezing Point Depression The amount of solute dissolved in a solvent affects the freezing point of the solvent. This special property of solutions is called **freezing point depression.** Adding solute lowers the freezing point of the solvent. The greater the amount of dissolved solute, the lower the freezing point of the solvent.

 PREDICT: What will happen to the freezing point of water as you add solute to the water?

Melting Danger Away Have you ever sprinkled rock salt or calcium chloride pellets on an icy sidewalk? Ice melters like these lower the freezing point of water. When the ice begins to melt, the chemical compounds dissolve in the water, forming solutions that freeze at a lower temperature than pure water.

Unfortunately, the use of salts for deicing can be hazardous to us and harmful to the environment. The salt residue that remains after the ice has melted can weaken pavement, forming potholes. In addition, chemicals wash off of paved surfaces into storm drains, increasing the salinity, or salt content, of nearby streams and lakes. Look at the differences among ice melters in the table in Figure 5-17.

ICE MELTERS		
Compound	Practical Melting Temperature	Advantages/Disadvantages
Rock salt (NaCl) Sodium chloride	−7° C	Abundant resource; pollutes streams and lakes; corrodes metal
Calcium chloride ($CaCl_2$)	−20° C	Abundant resource; may cause skin irritation; attacks concrete
Magnesium chloride ($MgCl_2$)	−15° C	Less toxic to plants and concrete surfaces than rock salts; leaves no powder residue
Calcium magnesium acetate (CMA)	−7° C	Less corrosive to automobiles and roads and less toxic to plants than other salts
Potassium chloride (KCl)	−11° C	Less toxic to plants and surfaces than rock salt; used in fertilizer so overuse may cause plants and grass to burn

▲ **Figure 5-17** The practical melting temperature is the lowest outdoor temperature for which each compound is effective. Below that temperature, the solution will start to freeze.

 PREDICT: What effects do you think the use of salts would have on plants and animals in the environment?

✔ CHECKING CONCEPTS

1. The _____ of pure water is 0°C.

2. The greater the amount of dissolved solute in a solvent, the _____ the freezing point of the solvent.

3. The freezing point of salt water is _____ than the freezing point of pure water.

4. Lowering the freezing point of a liquid solvent by adding solute is a property called _____.

5. Putting salt on icy roads _____ the freezing point of the melted ice.

THINKING CRITICALLY

6. **ANALYZE:** Beaker A contains 2 g of sugar dissolved in 100 mL of water. Beaker B contains 10 g of sugar dissolved in 100 mL of water. Which beaker contains the solution with the lower freezing point? Explain your answer.

7. **ANALYZE:** Beaker C and Beaker D each contain 5 g of dissolved copper sulfate. Beaker C contains 100 mL of water. Beaker D contains 250 mL of water. Which beaker contains the solution with the lower freezing point? Explain your answer.

Web InfoSearch

Salt and Ice Cream "I scream, you scream, we all scream for…" Rock salt is not only for deicing sidewalks. It can also be used to reduce the temperature of a container of juice, milk, or cream to make frozen desserts.

SEARCH: Use the Internet to find out about the history of the hand-cranked ice cream freezer. Describe its parts and how it can be used to make ice cream in a short report. Start your search at www.conceptsandchallenges.com. Some key search words are **Nancy Johnson** and **ice cream.**

Integrating Life Science

TOPICS: cold-blooded animals, circulation

FISH WITH ANTIFREEZE

Fish that live in the Arctic Ocean must survive freezing and near-freezing water temperatures. Scientists wondered why these fish did not freeze in such an environment.

By studying fish in the Arctic region of northern Labrador, scientists discovered that the blood of the Arctic fish contained a high concentration of a certain protein. This antifreeze protein (AFP) acts like a solute in a solution. The greater the amount of protein in the blood of the fish, the lower the freezing point of the blood.

As a result of this freezing point depression, the fish can survive in the cold Arctic environment. Should the water temperature reach 0°C, the blood of the fish would still be a liquid.

▲ **Figure 5-18** These fish can survive in subfreezing conditions.

Thinking Critically What helps fish live in such frigid water?

5-7 How do solutes affect boiling point?

Objective
Describe how a solute affects the boiling point of a solution.

Key Terms
boiling point: temperature at which a liquid changes to a gas

boiling point elevation: increase in the boiling point of a liquid solvent because of the addition of a solute

Boiling Point of Water When water is heated, its temperature rises. The temperature at which a liquid changes to a gas is called its **boiling point.** The boiling point of pure water at sea level is 100°C, at which point water changes to steam. Adding heat to boiling water does not raise its temperature.

Salt water does not boil at 100°C. This is because salt water contains dissolved salt particles. The particles of salt dissolved in the water interfere with the change from a liquid to a gas. The temperature of salt water must be higher than 100°C before the water will boil.

▶ **DESCRIBE:** What happens when the temperature of pure water reaches 100°C?

Boiling Point Elevation The boiling point of a liquid solvent is increased by adding a solute. This property of all solutions is called **boiling point elevation**. As the amount of solute in the solvent increases, the boiling point of the solvent also increases. For example, a solution of sugar and water does not boil at the same temperature as pure water because of boiling point elevation. Figure 5-20 lists some normal boiling points.

BOILING POINTS OF DIFFERENT SOLUTIONS	
Substance	Normal Boiling Point
Distilled water (at sea level)	100°C
Sea water	101°C
Vinegar	118°C
Ethyl alcohol	78.5°C
Acetone	56°C

▲ Figure 5-20

▶ **DEFINE:** What is boiling point elevation?

Keep That Engine Running Whenever the engine of a car is running, large amounts of heat are produced. A coolant is used to protect the engine from this heat. A coolant must also be able to remain liquid at low temperatures. The most common coolant is a solution of water and another liquid, usually ethylene glycol.

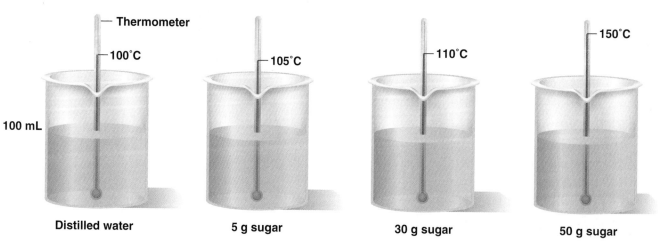

▲ **Figure 5-19** The boiling point of a solution increases as more solute is added.

Ethylene glycol freezes at –13°C and boils at 197°C. Although it is commonly called antifreeze, this compound could also be called antiboil because it lowers the freezing point of water and elevates its boiling point. In recent years, new antifreeze products have been developed. These products contain materials that are less toxic and safer for the environment than is ethylene glycol.

 DESCRIBE: What two important functions does an engine coolant have?

✓ CHECKING CONCEPTS

1. The _____ of pure water is 100°C.
2. The boiling point of salt water is _____ than the boiling point of pure water.
3. As the amount of solute in a solution increases, the boiling point of the solution _____.
4. Raising the boiling point of a liquid solvent by adding solute is called _____.

💡 THINKING CRITICALLY

5. **ANALYZE:** Solution A contains 5 g of sugar dissolved in 100 mL of water. Solution B contains 20 g of sugar dissolved in 100 mL of water. Which solution has the higher boiling point? Explain your answer.
6. **ANALYZE:** Two beakers each contain 12 g of salt dissolved in water. Beaker A contains 200 mL of water and Beaker B contains 100 mL of water. Which solution has the higher boiling point? Explain your answer.

DESIGNING AN EXPERIMENT

Design an experiment to solve the following problem. Include a hypothesis, variables, a procedure, and a type of data to study.

PROBLEM: How does the addition of salt to water affect the time it takes to boil an egg?

 Hands-On Activity

OBSERVING BOILING POINT ELEVATION

You will need three beakers, a thermometer, a heat source, a spoon, distilled water, and salt.

1. Put 100 mL of water in each beaker.
2. Add 5 g of salt to the first beaker and stir.
3. Heat the water in the beaker until it begins to boil. Record the temperature.
4. Add 10 g of salt to the second beaker and stir. Repeat Step 3.
5. Add 20 g of salt to the third beaker and stir. Repeat Step 3.

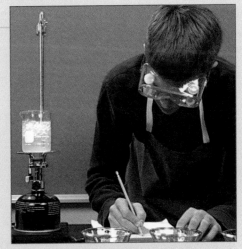
▲ **STEP 3** Heat the water until it begins to boil.

Practicing Your Skills

6. **OBSERVE:** What was the boiling point of the first solution?
7. **OBSERVE:** What was the boiling point of the second solution?
8. **OBSERVE:** What was the boiling point of the third solution?
9. **ANALYZE:** What is the relationship between the amount of a solute and the boiling point of a solution?

5-8 How can solutions be separated?

Objective

Describe two methods for separating the solute from the solvent in a solution.

Key Terms

evaporation (ee-vap-uh-RAY-shuhn): change from a liquid to a gas at the surface of the liquid

condensation (kahn-duhn-SAY-shuhn): change from a gas to a liquid

distillation (dihs-tuh-LAY-shuhn): process of evaporating a liquid and then condensing the gas back into a liquid

Evaporation A solute can be separated from a solution by evaporation. **Evaporation** is the change of a liquid to a gas at the surface of the liquid. The molecules at the surface of the liquid gain enough energy to break free of the liquid and move into the air as a gas.

You can separate copper sulfate crystals from a solution of copper sulfate and water. Place the solution in a shallow dish and let it stand. After a few days, all the water will have evaporated. Crystals of copper sulfate remain in the bottom of the dish.

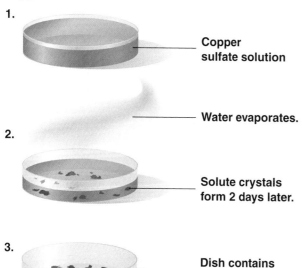

1.
Copper sulfate solution

2.
Water evaporates.

Solute crystals form 2 days later.

3.
Dish contains only crystals 4 days later.

▲ **Figure 5-21** The evaporation of a solvent leaves the solute.

1. INFER: How can you separate salt from saltwater?

Condensation Have you ever come out of a hot shower to find drops of water on your bathroom mirror? The drops of water are the result of condensation. **Condensation** is the change of a gas to a liquid. Some of the shower water evaporates to form water vapor, an invisible gas. When the water vapor strikes the mirror, it is cooled. This causes the water vapor to change back to liquid water.

2. DEFINE: What is condensation?

Distillation A liquid solution can be separated into its separate parts by the process of distillation. In the process of **distillation**, a liquid is heated until it evaporates. The gas is then cooled until it condenses back into a liquid.

When a solution is distilled, both the solvent and the solute can be recovered. The solution to be separated is heated. The solvent evaporates and forms a gas. The gas moves through a tube called a condenser. The condenser cools the gas, which changes back to a liquid. The liquid drips into a container. The solute remains in the original container. Both the solute and the solvent are recovered.

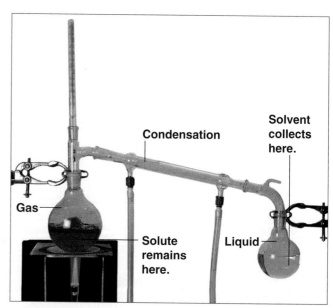

Condensation

Solvent collects here.

Gas

Solute remains here.

Liquid

▲ **Figure 5-22** Separation of a solution by distillation

3. IDENTIFY: What two processes are involved in distillation?

1. Evaporation changes a liquid to a _____ .

2. Condensation changes a gas to a _____ .

3. A solution can be separated into its solute and solvent by _____ .

4. As a liquid is heated, the molecules at the liquid's _____ evaporate first.

5. A solvent can be evaporated from a solution to recover the _____ .

6. Evaporation takes place at the _____ of a liquid.

7. During distillation, cooling the evaporated solute causes _____ to occur.

THINKING CRITICALLY

8. **INFER:** What causes steam to escape from the spout of a teakettle?

9. **HYPOTHESIZE:** Why do droplets of water form on the underside of the lid of a pot of boiling water?

BUILDING SCIENCE SKILLS

Researching Distillation can be used to purify water. Chemists and pharmacists use distilled water to make solutions. Distilled water is also used in car batteries. Use library references to find out how distilled water is prepared. Why is it sometimes important to use distilled water instead of ordinary tap water? Write a brief report of your findings.

Science and Technology

FRACTIONAL DISTILLATION OF PETROLEUM

Petroleum is a mixture of different substances. Gasoline, kerosene, and heating oil are just some of the products obtained from petroleum. Petroleum is separated by the process of fractional distillation. In this process, petroleum is heated in a fractionating (FRAK-shuhn-ayt-ing) tower. The different substances in petroleum have different boiling points. Each substance, or fraction, changes to a vapor at a different temperature. The process of fractional distillation depends on each substance's boiling point.

As the temperature in the fractionating tower increases, each substance changes to a vapor. The vapors pass through pipes where they cool and condense. Then, they collect separately. The substances with the highest boiling points cool and condense and drain from the lower part of the tower. These substances include asphalt and lubricating oil. Substances that boil at a lower temperature rise higher in the tower before they cool and condense. Fuel oil and kerosene drain off in the middle of the tower. Gasoline, with the lowest boiling point, rises to the top of the tower and drains off. Once the petroleum is separated into liquid fractions, each liquid drains into its storage tank.

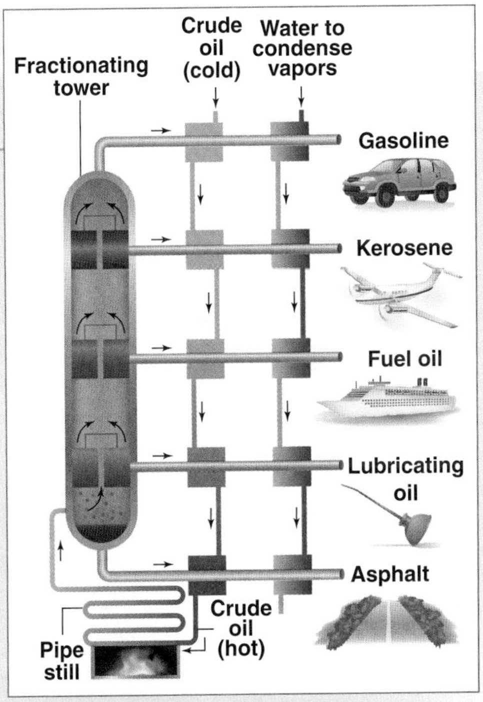

Thinking Critically Why do the substances with lower boiling points drain from the top of the tower, whereas those with higher boiling points drain from the bottom?

▲ Figure 5-23 Fractional distillation

LAB ACTIVITY
Making Supersaturated Solutions

Materials

Safety goggles,
lab apron, oven mitt,
heat source, marking
pen, 3 250-mL beakers,
100-mL graduated
cylinder,
glass stirrers,
3 plastic teaspoons,
water, sugar,
Epsom salt, table salt

BACKGROUND

The solubility of a solute is the amount of solute that will dissolve in a given amount of a certain solvent. This will produce a saturated solution. Increasing the temperature usually increases the solubility of a solute. To make a supersaturated solution, heat the solution, add more solute to it, and then cool it.

PURPOSE

In this activity, you will observe the solubility of different substances in solutions. Also, you will observe the relationship between solutes, solvents, and heat.

PROCEDURE

1. Copy the chart in Figure 5-24. Put on safety goggles and a lab apron.

2. Label each beaker with the following: table salt, Epsom salt, and sugar.

3. Add 100 mL of water to each beaker.

▲ STEP 2 Label each beaker.

Observing the Effects of Heat on a Solute and a Solvent			
Beaker	Solute	Number of Teaspoons to Make Saturated Solution	Number of Teaspoons After Heating
1	Table salt		
2	Epsom salt		
3	Sugar		

▲ **Figure 5-24** Copy this chart and use it to record your observations.

▲ **STEP 4** Make saturated solutions of each substance.

▲ **STEP 5** Place the beaker on the heat source and stir the contents.

4. Make saturated solutions of each substance. For each solution, add a teaspoonful of table salt, Epsom salt, or sugar to the corresponding beaker. Stir for one minute. Continue adding the solute and stirring until some does not dissolve. Record how many teaspoonfuls you add to make each saturated solution.

5. Place the beaker that contains table salt on a heat source. Stir the mixture with a glass stirrer as it is heating. As soon as the solid particles dissolve, add another teaspoon of table salt and stir. Add more table salt until some table salt is left behind. Record the number of teaspoons you add.
   ⚠ CAUTION: Be extremely careful when handling anything on a hot plate.

6. Allow the solution to cool. As it cools, record your observations.

7. Repeat Step 4 with the beakers that contain the Epsom salt and the sugar. Record your observations.

CONCLUSIONS

1. **OBSERVE:** Describe the appearance of the solutions at room temperature.

2. **OBSERVE:** Describe what happened to the solutions upon heating.

3. **INFER:** Which part of the activity represents a supersaturated solution? How do you know?

4. **ANALYZE:** How is the knowledge of solubility useful for people who make drink mixes or instant soups?

5-9 How are crystals formed?

Objective

Explain how crystals are formed from solutions.

Crystal Chemistry The particles that make up a crystal are arranged in a pattern. This pattern gives the crystal a definite shape. All crystals of the same substance have the same shape. Figure 5-25 shows how crystals of copper sulfate can "grow" from a saturated solution of this compound. As the saturated solution sits, water will evaporate. Copper sulfate crystals will appear in the bottom of the solution. These crystals will increase in size as more and more water evaporates.

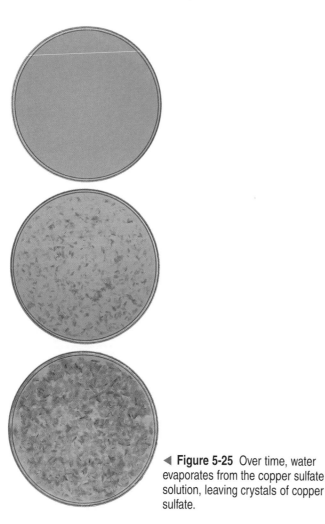

◀ **Figure 5-25** Over time, water evaporates from the copper sulfate solution, leaving crystals of copper sulfate.

▶ **INFER:** Why are all salt crystals shaped like a cube?

Seeding Another way to grow crystals is to use a supersaturated solution. Figure 5-26 shows how to grow crystals from a supersaturated solution of sodium acetate. After a saturated solution is prepared at a high temperature, let it cool to room temperature. Then add a small sodium acetate crystal to the solution. This sodium acetate "seed" causes the excess crystals of sodium acetate to come out of solution and settle quickly to the bottom of the container.

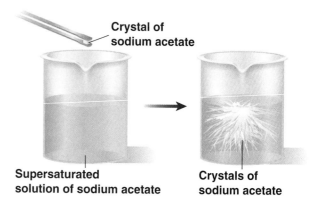

Crystal of sodium acetate

Supersaturated solution of sodium acetate

Crystals of sodium acetate

▲ **Figure 5-26** Growing sodium acetate crystals

▶ **DEFINE:** How does a supersaturated solution allow you to grow crystals?

Synthetic Crystals Natural crystals may contain flaws or impurities, but synthetic, or human-made, crystals can be made flawless. They can be made to grow in a particular shape or size to suit specific needs. Synthetic crystals are crucial to the development of new technology.

Optical crystals made of sodium chloride, potassium chloride, and many other crystalline compounds can be used in the development of laser and fiber-optic communication. Silicon chips are very thin slices of artificially grown silicon crystals. They are used in many electronic devices, such as the circuit boards of computers, to hold information and control mechanical functions. "Smart cards" are credit or debit cards that have a microprocessor built into the silicon chip on the card. These cards may be used in the future to store and update personal bank or credit account information.

Synthetic gems such as diamonds are used in industry primarily because of their strength and durability. Saws set with diamonds and diamond-tipped drill bits are

▲ Figure 5-27
A synthetic gem

used to cut and drill through glass, ceramics, and rocks. Because they do not corrode, diamonds are also used in medical instruments like diamond-bladed scalpels for eye surgery. Other types of gems can also be made with synthetic crystals.

3ᐅ LIST: What are some uses of synthetic crystals?

✓ CHECKING CONCEPTS

1. When water is evaporated from a copper sulfate solution, copper sulfate _____ remain.

2. All crystals of the same substance have the same _____.

3. A supersaturated solution contains more _____ than it would normally hold at a given temperature.

4. Crystals form when extra _____ is added to a supersaturated solution.

THINKING CRITICALLY

5. **PREDICT:** What will happen when sugar is added to a supersaturated solution of sugar and water?

BUILDING SCIENCE SKILLS

Organizing Information When you organize information, you put the information in some kind of order. Draw a chart showing the six basic crystal shapes. Use library references to identify a substance whose crystals have each type of shape.

Hands-On Activity

MAKING ROCK CANDY

You will need a sugar crystal, sugar-water solution prepared ahead of time, pencil, thread, large drinking glass, and paper towels.

1. From the container your teacher will supply, select a large sugar crystal. Remove it with tongs and dry it with a paper towel.

2. Pour some of the sugar-water solution from the container into a glass. Be careful not to pour any other crystals into the glass.

3. Tie one end of the thread to a pencil and the other end of the thread gently around the sugar crystal.

4. Balance the pencil over the opening of the glass so that the crystal is suspended in the solution. Do not let the crystal touch the bottom of the glass.

5. Let the glass sit undisturbed for several days to a week. Observe what grew on the string.

▲ **STEP 5** Observe the thread after a few days.

Practicing Your Skills

6. **OBSERVE:** What formed on the string after several days?

7. **HYPOTHESIZE:** What caused the result you observed?

THE Big IDEA

How are crystals formed on Earth?

Gases and liquids are disordered. The molecules in a liquid or a gas bounce off each other and flow. Think about some perfume evaporating from a liquid into a gas. The perfume vapor spreads out. Your nose can easily prove that molecules of perfume in a gas state have flowed all around the room.

Solids, however, do not flow. If you put a solid into an empty jar, it just sits at the bottom of the jar. It does not spread out or flow. The solid stays together because its molecules are often ordered in regular geometric patterns called crystals.

How do crystals form? When a substance cools from liquid to solid, its flowing molecules slow down. The molecules begin to line up, forming rows and layers. They pack together tightly to form a crystal.

Crystals can be found in many places. You can find crystals in a kitchen in the form of sugar and salt. Rock candy is a giant sugar crystal. Diamonds are very hard crystals of carbon. In the heart of a battery-powered watch is a quartz crystal, which vibrates when electricity flows through it. Crystals can form in volcanoes, teakettles, caves, and candy shops. Crystals form anywhere molecules line up in geometric rows and layers.

Look at the photos that appear on these two pages. Then, follow the directions in the Science Log to find out more about "the big idea." ✦

The Caverns of Sonora
These crystalline structures form in caves over thousands of years. They are deposits of minerals called calcite and aragonite, which come from water dripping into the cave. This close-up shows calcite crystals.

Volcanic eruption of Kilauea, Hawaii
Geodes are hollow rocks lined with crystals. Some geodes can form as a result of certain lava flows.

WRITING ACTIVITY

Science Log

Some crystals are as ordinary as table salt; others are as rare as priceless gems. Find out more about crystals. Then, in your science log, write an extraordinary story about a crystal. Start your search at www.conceptsandchallenges.com.

Kitchen Crystals
Sometime crystals form in teakettles. Minerals dissolved in water crystallize when the water boils and evaporates. This close-up shows these crystals.

Tufa Towers at Mono Lake, CA
The formations you see here are made as saltwater evaporates, leaving the salty towers. This close-up shows salt crystals.

Chapter 5 Challenges

Chapter Summary

Lesson 5-1

- When a substance dissolves, it goes into **solution**, a mixture in which one substance is evenly mixed with another substance.

Lesson 5-2

- The substance that dissolves in a solution is called the **solute**. The **solvent** is the substance in which a solute dissolves.
- A substance that dissolves in another substance is **soluble** in that substance.

Lesson 5-3

- A molecule is polar if one end has a positive charge and the other end has a negative charge.
- Water is called the universal solvent because it can dissolve many different substances.

Lesson 5-4

- Stirring, crushing, or heating a solvent increases the rate at which a solute dissolves.

Lesson 5-5

- An **unsaturated solution** contains less solute than it can hold at a given temperature.
- A **saturated solution** contains all the solute it can hold at a given temperature.

Lesson 5-6

- Lowering the **freezing point** of a liquid solvent by adding solute is called **freezing point depression**.

Lesson 5-7

- The temperature at which a liquid changes to a gas is called its **boiling point**. Raising the boiling point of a liquid solvent by adding solute is called **boiling point elevation.**

Lesson 5-8

- **Evaporation** is the process by which a liquid changes to a gas at the surface of the liquid.
- **Condensation** is the process by which a gas changes to a liquid.

Lesson 5-9

- Crystals form when extra solute is added to a supersaturated solution.

Key Term Challenges

boiling point (p. 116)
boiling point
  elevation (p. 116)
concentrated solution
  (p. 112)
condensation (p. 118)
dilute solution (p. 112)
dissolve (p.104)
distillation (p. 118)
evaporation (p. 118)
freezing point (p. 114)
freezing point
  depression (p. 114)
insoluble (p. 106)
polar molecule (p. 108)
saturated solution (p. 112)
solubility (p. 106)
soluble (p. 106)
solute (p. 106)
solution (p. 104)
solvent (p. 106)
supersaturated
  solution (p. 112)
unsaturated solution
  (p. 112)

MATCHING **Write the Key Term from above that best matches each description.**

1. temperature at which a liquid changes to a solid

2. solution containing more solute than it can normally hold at a given temperature

3. change of a gas to a liquid

4. temperature at which a liquid changes to a gas

5. lowering the freezing point of a liquid solvent by adding solute

6. solution containing less solute than it can hold at a given temperature

FILL IN **Write the Key Term from above that best completes each statement.**

7. Extra solute sitting at the bottom of a solution indicates the solution is a _____.

8. Increasing the amount of solute in a solution can make a _____.

9. In distillation of a liquid, _____ occurs first and then condensation.

10. For a solution to form, a _____ must dissolve in a solvent.

11. Powdered sugar _____ faster than a sugar cube.

12. The _____ of pure water is 0°C.

Content Challenges ~~TEST PREP~~

MULTIPLE CHOICE **Write the letter of the term or phrase that best completes each statement.**

1. Extra solute sitting at the bottom of a solution indicates the solution is _____.
   a. dilute
   b. unsaturated
   c. saturated
   d. supersaturated

2. As the amount of solute in a solution increases, the _____ of the solution also increases.
   a. boiling point
   b. temperature
   c. freezing point
   d. solubility

3. In distillation, a liquid _____ and then condenses.
   a. sublimes
   b. freezes
   c. boils
   d. evaporates

4. For a solution to form, a _____ must dissolve in a solvent.
   a. chemical
   b. solute
   c. soda
   d. salt

5. Crystals of the same substance have the same _____.
   a. shape
   b. size
   c. faces
   d. irregularities

6. Powdered sugar dissolves _____ a sugar cube.
   a. more slowly than
   b. at the same rate as
   c. faster than
   d. the same way as

7. The _____ of pure water is 0°C.
   a. boiling point
   b. freezing point
   c. room temperature
   d. solubility

8. Adding antifreeze to a car's cooling system raises the _____ of the water it contains.
   a. amount
   b. freezing point
   c. concentration
   d. boiling point

9. Placing rock salt on an icy sidewalk lowers the _____ of melted ice.
   a. evaporation
   b. freezing point
   c. boiling point
   d. condensation

10. A _____ solution contains more solute than it can normally hold at a given temperature.
    a. dilute
    b. supersaturated
    c. unsaturated
    d. saturated

TRUE/FALSE **Write *true* if the statement is true. If the statement is false, change the underlined term to make the statement true.**

11. Stirring a solution <u>speeds up</u> the rate at which a solute dissolves.

12. The freezing point of salt water is <u>higher</u> than that of pure water.

13. Crystals form when extra solute is added to <u>an unsaturated</u> solution.

14. The ends of a water molecule are <u>electrically charged</u>.

15. As the amount of solute in a solution increases, the boiling point of the solution <u>decreases</u>.

Concept Challenges TEST PREP

WRITTEN RESPONSE Complete the exercises and answer each of the following questions in complete sentences.

1. **ANALYZE:** The law of conservation of matter states that matter cannot be created or destroyed but only changed from one form to another. How does the evaporation of water support this law?

2. **COMPARE:** Compare the effect of an increased amount of solute on both the boiling point and the freezing point of a solution.

3. **INFER:** How could information about crystal shape be used to identify an unknown substance?

4. **HYPOTHESIZE:** What effect does evaporation have on Earth's oceans?

5. **EXPLAIN:** Club soda contains carbon dioxide gas dissolved in liquid water. Explain why a bottle of club soda goes "flat" when it is left open at room temperature.

INTERPRETING A GRAPH Use Figure 5-28 to answer the following questions. Round off your numbers.

6. About how many grams of sodium nitrate can be dissolved in 100 g of water at a temperature of 50°C?

7. At what temperature will 100 g of water dissolve 160 g of sodium nitrate?

8. About how much sodium nitrate can be dissolved in 100 g of water at a temperature equal to the boiling point of pure water?

9. About how much sodium nitrate can be dissolved in 100 g of water at a temperature equal to the freezing point of pure water?

10. What is the relationship between the temperature of a solvent and the amount of solute it can dissolve?

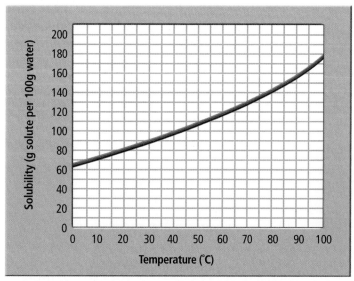

▲ **Figure 5-28** Graph showing the solubility of sodium nitrate

Chapter 6 Suspensions

▲ **Figure 6-1** A decorative, stained-glass window

Stained glass is used to decorate because light shines through, making colors look as if they are glowing. It is used in windows, lamp shades, and sculptures.

Clear glass is an unusual solution in which particles of sand and other substances are evenly mixed. Stained glass is different. It is actually a mixture in which color particles are suspended within the clear glass. The color particles are actually minerals. Cobalt makes blues. Copper makes greens and reds.

►What is the difference between the particles in two different colors?

Contents

6-1 What is a suspension?

Objective
Describe the characteristics of a suspension.

Key Term
suspension (suh-SPEHN-shuhn): mixture of two materials or more that separate on standing

Suspensions If you add some soil to a jar of water, the water will become cloudy. If you let the mixture stand, you will notice that the soil particles settle to the bottom of the jar. A mixture of soil and water is an example of a suspension. A **suspension** is a mixture of two or more materials that separate on standing. An important thing to remember about suspensions is that most types of suspensions are temporary. The materials in an ordinary suspension may appear to be well mixed at first, but in time they will separate.

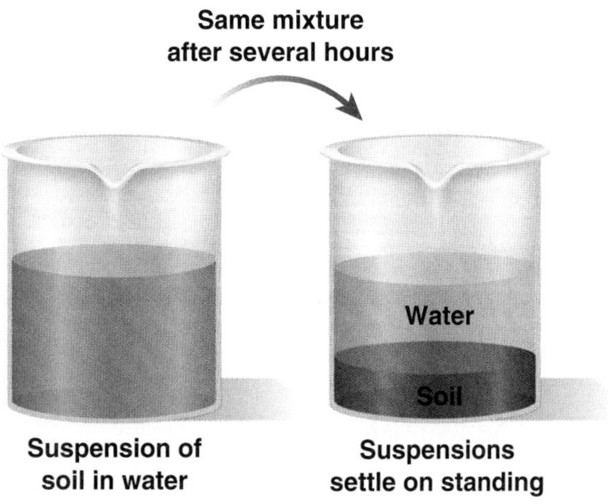

Same mixture after several hours

Suspension of soil in water

Suspensions settle on standing

▲ **Figure 6-2** Soil and water make a temporary suspension.

In many cases the particles of a suspension will separate into layers. Think about a suspension of soil and water. If you were to examine this mixture after it has separated, you would notice that the soil has formed definite layers. Soil is made up of particles of different sizes and weights. As the particles settle, they form layers, with the heaviest particles on the bottom and the lightest particles on top.

▶ **DEFINE:** What is a suspension?

Particles in Suspensions The particles in a solution are much too small to be seen, even with the aid of a microscope. That is because the particles in a solution are mixed at the smallest level possible—as atoms or molecules. However, the particles in a suspension are much larger. You can see the particles in some suspensions without a microscope. In other suspensions, the particles are visible with a microscope.

▶ **COMPARE:** How does the size of the particles in a suspension compare with the size of the particles in a solution?

Properties of Suspensions An important property of suspensions is that the particles of a suspension scatter light. You can observe this property by darkening a room and shining a flashlight through a mixture of soil and water. The beam of light will be visible as it passes through the cloudy water. One way that you can tell the difference between a solution and a suspension is that the particles of a solution do not scatter light. Figure 6-3 compares some properties of solutions and suspensions.

PROPERTIES OF SOLUTIONS AND SUSPENSIONS	
Solution	Suspension
Mixture	Mixture
Clear	Cloudy
Particles evenly mixed	Particles settle on standing
Particles too small to be seen	Particles can be seen

▲ **Figure 6-3** Compare the properties of solutions and suspensions.

▶ **OBSERVE:** What property do suspensions and solutions have in common?

Examples of Suspensions A familiar example of a suspension is an oil and vinegar salad dressing. If you shake a bottle of salad dressing, the contents mix together. Once you put the bottle down, however, the ingredients separate. That is why the labels on bottles of salad dressing often state "Shake well before using."

Not all suspensions involve liquids. A common suspension of a solid in a gas is dust or smoke particles suspended in the air. Smog, a suspension of smoke and fog in air, is a common pollutant. Clouds, another suspension, are made up of tiny particles of water or ice suspended in air.

▲ Figure 6-4 A dust storm is a suspension of a solid in a gas.

 LIST: What are two common examples of suspensions?

✓ CHECKING CONCEPTS

1. If a suspension is allowed to stand, the substances will _____.
2. The appearance of a _____ is cloudy.
3. The _____ in a suspension are larger than atoms or molecules.
4. An example of a suspension of a solid in a gas is _____ suspended in air.
5. Solutions and suspensions are similar in that both are _____.

💡 THINKING CRITICALLY

6. **CONTRAST:** How are the particles in a suspension different from those in a solution?
7. **CLASSIFY:** Look at Figure 6-3. Are the properties listed physical or chemical properties?

BUILDING SCIENCE SKILLS

Analyzing Prepare mixtures of each of the following in water: salt, sand, pepper, and sugar. Stir each mixture and use what you have learned to decide whether each mixture is a solution or a suspension. Record all your observations and tell how you reached your conclusions.

 Hands-On Activity

MAKING A SUSPENSION

You will need safety goggles, water, vegetable oil, starch, a spoon, and two small jars with lids.

1. Put on the goggles. Half-fill each jar with water.
2. To one jar, add two spoonfuls of starch.
3. Add vegetable oil to the other jar until it is about two-thirds full.
4. Put the lids tightly on both jars.
5. Shake each jar for about 30 seconds.
6. Allow the jars to remain still for five minutes.

▲ STEP 5 Shake each jar.

Practicing Your Skills

7. **EXPLAIN:** Why did you shake the jars?
8. **OBSERVE:** What happened when you allowed the jars to sit?
9. **ANALYZE:** Are both of the mixtures you made suspensions? How do you know?

6-2 How can a suspension be separated?

STEP 2

Objective

Describe some ways to separate a suspension.

Key Terms

filtration: separation of particles in a suspension by passing the suspension through filter paper or some other porous material

coagulation (koh-ag-yoo-LAY-shuhn)**:** use of chemicals to make the particles in a suspension clump together

Settling   Particles in a suspension settle on standing. Large particles settle out quickly. Smaller particles take a longer time to settle. You can see how this works in Figure 6-5.

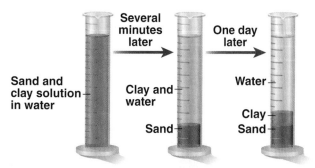

▲ Figure 6-5 Suspensions separate on standing.

1▶ EXPLAIN: When sand and clay are mixed with water, which settles faster? Explain.

Filtration   **Filtration** is the removal of particles in a suspension by passing the suspension through a filter. Filters can be made of paper, charcoal, or other materials. Filters are porous. They have tiny openings, or pores, through which some materials can pass and some cannot. Materials that cannot pass through the filter have particles that are larger than the pores in the filter.

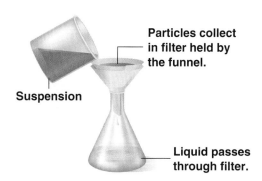

▲ Figure 6-6 Suspensions can be separated by filtration.

2▶ PREDICT: What happens to particles in a suspension that are larger than the pores in a filter?

Coagulation   Another way to separate a suspension is to add chemicals that make the particles of the suspension stick together. The particles form clumps that are larger and heavier than the original particles. As a result, the particles settle out more quickly. This process is called **coagulation.** Alum is a common coagulant. Coagulation takes place when you cut your finger. Chemicals in your blood cause the blood to coagulate and form a clot.

 DEFINE: What is coagulation?

Spinning A fourth way to separate a suspension is to spin a mixture at high speeds. The device used to spin a mixture is called a centrifuge (SEN-truh-fyooj). As the suspension is spun around, the particles in the suspension are pulled to the bottom of the container. Use of a centrifuge greatly increases the rate at which a suspension separates. The solid materials in blood cells are separated from the liquid materials, the plasma, by centrifugation.

 IDENTIFY: What is a centrifuge?

 CHECKING CONCEPTS

1. What happens when a suspension is left to stand overnight?
2. What is filtration?

3. What is coagulation?
4. How is a centrifuge used to separate the particles in a suspension?

 THINKING CRITICALLY

5. **ANALYZE:** Which method of separating a suspension is described? **a.** A solution of ammonium hydroxide and alum is added to a clay-and-water suspension. **b.** A suspension is passed through a piece of linen cloth.

BUILDING SCIENCE SKILLS

Modeling Make a model to show how coagulation works. Half-fill two test tubes with water. Add a small amount of clay to each. To one of the test tubes, add several drops of alum solution. Then, add several drops of ammonium hydroxide to the same test tube. Observe both test tubes for several minutes. In the test tube that you added the alum solution and the ammonium hydroxide, you should see a jellylike material form. This causes the clay particles to clump together. In which test tube do the clay particles settle faster? Why?

Integrating Earth Science

TOPICS: sediments, rivers, erosion

THE MISSISSIPPI DELTA

As a river flows, it carries particles of clay, sand, and gravel. These particles are called sediments. The sediments are suspended in the water.

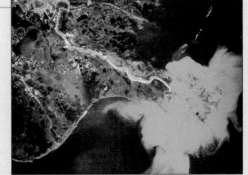

▲ **Figure 6-7** Aerial view of Mississippi delta

A river picks up sediments as it floods and erodes its banks. A fast-moving river carries the most sediments. As the banks of a river widen, the river slows down. When the river slows down, sediments settle out of the suspension and are deposited. Rocks and pebbles are deposited first because they are the heaviest and largest particles. Sand has the next largest particles. Silt and clay, having the smallest particles, are deposited last.

The widest part of a river is usually its mouth, where it empties into a larger body of water. The Mississippi River's mouth is located at the Gulf of Mexico. Here, the Mississippi moves so slowly that sediments from the river are deposited. Gradually, the sediments form new land called a delta. The land of the Mississippi delta is good for farming because new topsoil is always being deposited.

Thinking Critically Why do you think materials are deposited in the order given above?

6-3 What is an emulsion?

Objective

Describe and give examples of an emulsion.

Key Terms

emulsion (ee-MUL-shuhn): suspension of two liquids

homogenization (huh-mahj-uh-nih-ZAY-shuhn): formation of a permanent emulsion

Emulsions When a liquid is suspended in another liquid, the result is an **emulsion.** Milk, paint, and many medicines are examples of emulsions.

You can make an emulsion by mixing some cooking oil with water, and then shaking the mixture. This emulsion will not stay mixed for long. If you let the mixture stand, the oil and water will soon separate. An emulsion that does not stay mixed is called a temporary emulsion.

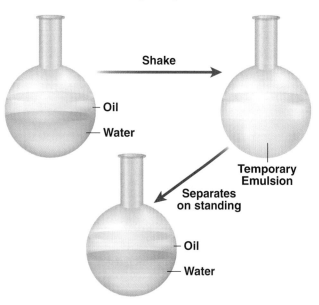

Shake

Oil
Water

Temporary Emulsion

Separates on standing

Oil

Water

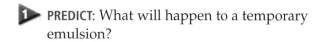

▲ **Figure 6-8** A temporary emulsion separates on standing.

▶ **PREDICT:** What will happen to a temporary emulsion?

Permanent Emulsions Many types of commercial products that are emulsions do not separate on standing. These emulsions are called permanent emulsions. The particles in a permanent emulsion are much smaller than the particles in a temporary emulsion. The particles in a permanent emulsion are small enough to stay in suspension.

A familiar example of a permanent emulsion is homogenized milk. **Homogenization** is the formation of a permanent emulsion. Fresh milk is a temporary emulsion that quickly separates into milk and cream. Fresh milk is homogenized in a machine that breaks down the cream into very small particles. The small particles of cream remain permanently suspended in the milk.

▲ **Figure 6-9** The fresh milk coming from these cows is a temporary emulsion.

2 **CONTRAST:** What is the difference between a temporary emulsion and a permanent emulsion?

Emulsifying Agents Many detergents or other cleaning products contain substances called emulsifying agents. An emulsifying agent keeps an emulsion from separating. The soap in cleaning products is an emulsifying agent. Soap breaks apart grease or dirt into smaller particles. These particles are small enough to form a permanent emulsion with water. The dirt or grease is washed away in the water.

Other emulsifying agents include gelatin and egg yolk. These substances are often used in food to keep ingredients from separating.

3 IDENTIFY: What is an emulsifying agent?

✔ CHECKING CONCEPTS

1. An emulsion is a suspension of a _____ in a liquid.
2. Oil and water separate on standing because they form a _____ emulsion.
3. The particles in a _____ emulsion are small enough to stay in suspension.
4. Soap is an example of an _____ agent.
5. Milk and cream form a permanent emulsion through the process of _____.

THINKING CRITICALLY

6. HYPOTHESIZE: Bile is produced by the liver. It emulsifies the fats that a person eats. Why is this process important to the digestive process?

7. INFER: When you buy a can of paint, you usually have to stir the paint before you can use it. Why do you think it is necessary to stir the paint?

Web InfoSearch

Homogenization Fresh milk right from a cow is a temporary emulsion. It separates on standing into cream and milk. Before it is sold in stores, the milk is homogenized, making it a permanent emulsion.

SEARCH: Use the Internet to find out how milk is homogenized. Create a poster to show the steps. Start your search at www.conceptsandchallenges.com. Some key search words are **milk** and **homogenize.**

Hands-On Activity

MAKING AN EMULSION

You will need safety goggles, vinegar, vegetable oil, an egg, a bowl, a measuring cup, and an eggbeater.

1. Separate the yolk from the white of the egg. Put the yolk in the bowl.
2. Beat the egg yolk until it looks foamy.
3. Add 1/4 cup of vinegar to the egg yolk. Beat the mixture of vinegar and egg yolk.
4. Add 1/8 cup of oil to the mixture one tablespoon at a time. Beat the mixture thoroughly each time you add a tablespoon of oil.

▲ STEP 2 Beat the egg yolk.

Practicing Your Skills

5. OBSERVE: When did the mixture begin to thicken?
6. PREDICT: If the mixture is allowed to stand, will it separate?
7. ANALYZE: What is the emulsifying agent in the mixture?
8. PREDICT: What would happen if you did not add the egg yolk to the mixture?

6-4 What is a colloid?

Objective
Describe and give examples of a colloid.

Key Term
colloid (KAHL-oid): suspension in which the particles are permanently suspended

Colloids What do whipped cream, fog, mayonnaise, and smoke have in common? All of these substances are colloids. A **colloid** is a suspension in which the particles are permanently suspended. Colloids can be mixtures of different phases of matter. Figure 6-10 shows some common types of colloids and examples of each type.

 DEFINE: What is a colloid?

Colloid Particle Size The particles in a colloid are not as small as the particles in a solution. However, they are much smaller than the particles in an ordinary suspension. They cannot be seen with an ordinary microscope. Because the particles are so small, a colloid cannot be separated by normal means of filtration. A colloid such as homogenized milk passes right through filter paper. The particles in milk are smaller than the pores in the filter.

 EXPLAIN: Why can a colloid not be separated by filtration?

Movement of Colloid Particles Have you ever traveled in a car on a foggy night? If so, you probably know that the car's headlight beams do not penetrate very far into the fog. Fog is a colloid made up of tiny water droplets suspended in air. When light passes through fog, the light strikes these droplets and is scattered, or spreads out. This scattering of light by the particles of a colloid is known as the Tyndall effect.

▲ **Figure 6-11** Light passes through a solution (right) but is scattered by a colloid (left).

Why do the particles of a colloid not settle out, much like the particles do in an ordinary suspension? After all, there is no emulsifying agent keeping them in suspension. The answer is that the very tiny particles of a colloid are constantly bumping into molecules of the surrounding material. For example, the water droplets in fog keep colliding with air molecules. These collisions keep the droplets from settling out of the colloid.

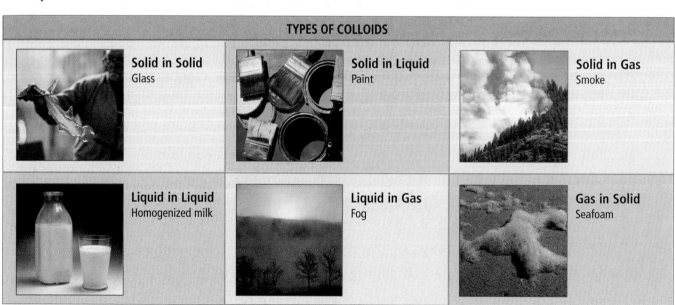

TYPES OF COLLOIDS

Solid in Solid
Glass

Solid in Liquid
Paint

Solid in Gas
Smoke

Liquid in Liquid
Homogenized milk

Liquid in Gas
Fog

Gas in Solid
Seafoam

▲ Figure 6-10

Instead, the droplets move rapidly through the air with a zigzag motion. When light passes through a colloid, it strikes the moving particles and is scattered, or spreads out. The cloudy appearance of a colloid is caused by the scattering of light.

3 ▶ EXPLAIN: Why does a colloid appear cloudy?

✓ CHECKING CONCEPTS

1. How do the particles in a colloid compare in size with those in a solution?

2. Are colloids permanent or temporary suspensions?

3. What happens if a colloid is passed through a filter?

4. What happens to light that passes through a colloid?

5. Give an example of a colloid consisting of a solid in a liquid.

💡 THINKING CRITICALLY

6. INFER: Why can the beam of a flashlight be seen as it passes through a bowl of gelatin?

7. COMPARE: In what ways are colloids like solutions? In what ways are they different?

8. EXPLAIN: How is paint made that it can be classified as a colloid?

Web InfoSearch

Brownian Motion If you look at a colloid through a very powerful microscope, you will see that the particles of a colloid are in continuous random motion. This motion is called Brownian motion. Brownian motion is named for the biologist Robert Brown. Brown first noticed this motion while observing the motion of particles in a suspension of pollen grains in water.

SEARCH: Use the Internet to find out more about Brownian motion and the scientist who first noticed it. Write a short report. Start your search at www.conceptsandchallenges.com. Some key search words are **Robert Brown, biologist**, and **Brownian motion**.

Science and Technology

USE OF COLLOIDS TO PURIFY WATER

Do you know where your household water comes from? In many cases, the water you use in your home comes from wells or reservoirs some distance from your house. Before this water reaches your house, it goes to a treatment plant. At the treatment plant, the water passes through several stages before it is clean enough for people to use.

Water from wells or reservoirs is passed through screens, which remove debris. Then, the water is sent to tanks or ponds where suspended materials are allowed to settle. Even after settling has taken place, some fine particles still remain suspended. At one time, these fine particles were allowed to remain in the water. Today, colloids are used to trap and remove these undesirable materials from our drinking water. Next, the water is filtered through sand or charcoal. Then it is pumped to sprinklers that spray the water into the air. This aerated water is then treated with chemicals to purify it before it is sent to our homes.

Thinking Critically Which stage in water treatment removes the largest particles?

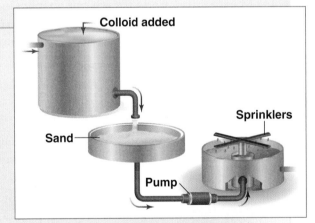

▲ Figure 6-12 Colloids are used to help purify water.

THE Big IDEA

What suspensions, emulsions, or colloids do you eat?

You have learned that a solution is a mixture in which substances are evenly mixed. The dissolved particles in a solution are about the size of molecules. If a solution of salt water sits for 100 years without evaporating, the salt stays dissolved. Not all mixtures are solutions. A suspension is a cloudy mixture of different substances.

The Food Guide Pyramid is a guide to good nutrition. It reflects the findings of research on nutrition. The right amount of foods from each group is recommended for a balanced, healthy diet on a daily basis. Many of the foods we eat are suspensions, emulsion, or colloids. They are from different parts of the Food Guide Pyramid.

Salad dressing and split pea soup are suspensions. In a suspension, the particles in the mixture are big enough to be separated by gravity or by filtering. An emulsion is a special kind of suspension made from two liquids that are permanently mixed. Ever had an emulsion for breakfast? Milk is a delicious and nutritious emulsion. Eggs are the emulsifiers in some products, such as mayonnaise.

Permanent suspensions are called colloids. In a colloid, the particles are so tiny that they stay mixed. Flavored gelatin and whipped cream are tasty colloids.

Look at the illustrations, photographs, and text that appear on these two pages. Then, follow the directions in the Science Log to learn more about "the big idea." ✦

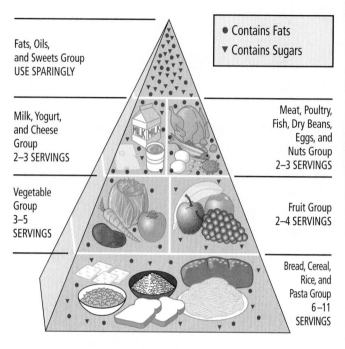

- • Contains Fats
- ▼ Contains Sugars

Fats, Oils, and Sweets Group
USE SPARINGLY

Milk, Yogurt, and Cheese Group
2–3 SERVINGS

Meat, Poultry, Fish, Dry Beans, Eggs, and Nuts Group
2–3 SERVINGS

Vegetable Group
3–5 SERVINGS

Fruit Group
2–4 SERVINGS

Bread, Cereal, Rice, and Pasta Group
6–11 SERVINGS

▲ **Figure 6-13** The Food Guide Pyramid shows what you should eat every day for a healthy diet.

Temporary Suspension

A soup, such as this one, is a mixture of many ingredients. A serving of soup contains several food groups, such as vegetables, proteins, and grains.

Emulsion

The egg yolks in mayonnaise keep the molecules of oil mixed with molecules of water. The egg yolks in mayonnaise function as emulsifiers. Because of its fat content, you should not eat too much mayonnaise.

Emulsion

Milk, fresh from a cow, separates into cream and milk. Milk that you buy in a store does not separate because it has been homogenized. The cream and the milk are permanently mixed. This emulsion is an important part of a healthy diet. 3–4 servings a day are recommended.

Colloid

Whipped cream is a colloid made by mixing gas into liquid cream. Cream is part of the milk and dairy group. Because it is high in fat, cream should be eaten sparingly. If you eat a small amount of it with a cup of strawberries, you have a healthy colloid-topped snack.

Temporary Suspension

A salad dressing with vinegar and oil is a suspension that will separate quickly. The harder it is shaken, the smaller the particles become, and the longer it remains mixed. A small amount of this suspension on a salad is part of a healthy diet.

WRITING ACTIVITY

Science Log

Many foods are suspensions. Pick a suspension that you enjoy eating and research how to make it. Describe other foods that you like to eat with the suspension. Here are some examples of foods that are suspensions: split pea soup, tomato sauce, applesauce, salad dressing, mayonnaise, whipped cream, butter, and jelly. Start your search at www.conceptsandchallenges.com.

6-5 What are air and water pollution?

Objective
Describe some causes of air and water pollution.

Key Terms
pollution (puh-LOO-shuhn)**:** release of harmful substances into the environment

potable (POHT-uh-buhl) **water:** water that is safe to drink

Pollution   What would happen if you did not have clean air to breathe or clean water to drink? One thing that would happen is that your health would be harmed. Every day our air and water resources are being threatened by pollution. **Pollution** is the adding of harmful substances, called pollutants, to the environment. Pollutants may be solids, liquids, or gases.

▶ **1** **DEFINE:** What are pollutants?

Causes of Pollution   Most pollution is caused by human activities. Exhaust from cars, trucks, and buses is a major source of air pollution. Waste products from factories pollute air, land, and water. Burning fossil fuels releases harmful gases into the atmosphere.

▶ **2** **LIST:** What are three sources of pollution?

Safe Water   There are many sources of water pollution. Agricultural use of pesticides and fertilizers is one major source. Another is the release of sewage and chemical wastes into rivers and lakes by cities and towns, factories, and even by individuals. Nuclear power plants release very hot water into nearby sources of water. This heats a river or stream to higher than normal temperatures. These pollutants harm fish and other organisms that live in the water. They also make the water unsafe to drink.

Water that is safe to drink is called **potable water.** Water can be made potable when it is passed through a series of steps in a process called purification (pyoor-uh-fih-KAY-shuhn). One of the steps is to add chemicals, such as chlorine, to kill germs. Other steps include settling, coagulation, and filtration. These steps remove solid particles that are suspended in water.

▶ **3** **IDENTIFY:** What is potable water?

Reducing Air Pollution   Air pollution can be harmful to people in many ways. Gases and solid particles in the air can cause irritation of the eyes, nose, and throat. They can cause breathing problems and respiratory illness.

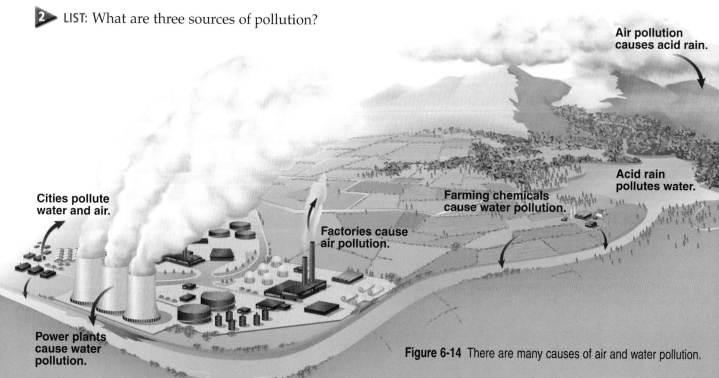

Air pollution causes acid rain.

Acid rain pollutes water.

Cities pollute water and air.

Factories cause air pollution.

Farming chemicals cause water pollution.

Power plants cause water pollution.

Figure 6-14 There are many causes of air and water pollution.

▲ **Figure 6-15** Air pollution over Montreal, Canada

Everyone can help to reduce air pollution. You can ride a bike or walk short distances instead of using a car or a bus. You might join a car pool with friends to help reduce the number of cars on the road. By lowering the temperature in your home, your family can use less heating oil. Find out what else you can do to help reduce air pollution.

 INFER: How would fewer cars on the road help to reduce air pollution?

✓ CHECKING CONCEPTS

1. Substances that are harmful to the environment are _____ .
2. Using less fuel to heat your home helps to reduce _____ pollution.
3. Water that is safe to drink is called _____ .
4. Chemical wastes and sewage are major causes of _____ pollution.

THINKING CRITICALLY

5. **HYPOTHESIZE:** Often trees that are planted along city streets do not grow well. What is a possible reason for this?

HEALTH AND SAFETY TIP

Never drink the water in a stream or brook. It may be polluted with chemicals or bacteria. Use library references to find out how you can purify water to make it safe for you to drink.

Hands-On Activity

OBSERVING POLLUTANTS IN AIR

You will need glass slides, petroleum jelly, and a hand lens.

1. Coat one side of several glass slides with a thin layer of petroleum jelly.
2. Choose several indoor and outdoor spots for testing the air quality.
3. At each spot, place a slide with the coated side up.
4. Record the location and the time when you placed each slide. Leave the slides overnight.
5. Collect the slides the next day. Record the time of collection.
6. Using the hand lens, examine each slide. Record your observations.

▲ **STEP 6** Examine each slide with a hand lens.

Practicing Your Skills

7. **OBSERVE:** What kinds of particles did you see on the slides?
8. **OBSERVE:** Which slide had the most particles?
9. **OBSERVE:** Which slide had the fewest particles?
10. **HYPOTHESIZE:** How can you explain your results?

LAB ACTIVITY
Testing for the Tyndall Effect— Solution or Nonsolution?

Materials List

Goggles, apron,
6 jars with lids,
flashlight, funnel
rubbing alcohol,
black construction paper,
sharpened pencil,
powdered juice mix,
sugar, sand, whole milk,
vegetable oil, water,
10 mL and 100 mL
graduated cylinders,
teaspoon, eyedropper

▲ **STEP 2** Add mixtures to the jars labeled A–F.

▲ **STEP 3** Shake the jars with the mixtures.

BACKGROUND

Some mixtures that may appear to look like a solution may not be one after all. Some of these "nonsolutions" may be suspensions or colloids. If a path of light can be seen easily through a mixture, then the mixture is not a solution. This happens because the particles are large enough to scatter or reflect the light. This light scattering is called the Tyndall effect.

PURPOSE

In this activity, you will make various mixtures and observe the difference between solutions and non-solutions using the Tyndall effect.

PROCEDURE

1. Copy the chart in Figure 6-16. Put on safety goggles and a lab apron.

2. Label the jars A through F for the following mixtures to be tested:

   A. 1 teaspoon of powdered juice mix to 100 mL of water

   B. 10 mL of rubbing alcohol to 100 mL of water

   C. 5 drops of whole milk to 100 mL of water

   D. 1 teaspoon of sugar to 100 mL of water

   E. 10 mL of vegetable oil to 100 mL of water

   F. 1 teaspoon of sand to 100 mL of water

3. Shake each jar and observe the mixtures. Predict which mixtures will be solutions or nonsolutions.

4. Make a solution tester. First cut out a small circle from a piece of black construction paper. The circle should just cover the lens of the flashlight. Use a sharpened pencil to punch a small hole in the center of the circle. Then, tape the paper circle over the flashlight lens.

5. In a darkened area of the room, press the solution tester very close to the jar holding mixture A. Record what you see. If you can see the path of light through the mixture, it is not a true solution.

6. Repeat Step 5 for mixtures B–F. Record your results.

▲ **STEP 5** Shine the solution tester into the jar.

Testing for the Tyndall Effect—Solution or Nonsolution?

Beaker	Mixture	Observations Upon Mixing	Observations When Testing With Solution Tester
A	Powdered juice mix and water		
B	Rubbing alcohol and water		
C	Whole milk and water		
D	Sugar and water		
E	Vegetable oil and water		
F	Sand and water		

▲ **Figure 6-16** Copy this chart and use it to record your observations.

CONCLUSIONS

1. **OBSERVE:** Describe what you observed with each mixture.

2. **MODEL:** Which mixtures represented solutions? How do you know?

3. **MODEL:** Which mixtures represented nonsolutions?

4. **INFER:** Explain how the nonsolutions show the Tyndall effect.

5. **ANALYZE:** How might you be able to determine if the nonsolutions are suspensions or colloids?

Chapter 6 Challenges

Chapter Summary

Lesson 6-1

- A **suspension** is a mixture of two or more substances that settle out over time.
- The particles in a suspension are larger than the particles in a solution.
- The particles in a suspension scatter light.
- Some familiar examples of suspensions include salad dressing and dust in the air.

Lesson 6-2

- The particles in a suspension settle out.
- **Filtration** is a method of separating a suspension by passing it through a filter.
- **Coagulation** is a process in which chemicals are used to make the particles in a suspension clump together.
- A centrifuge is a device that separates a suspension by spinning it at high speeds.

Lesson 6-3

- An **emulsion** is a suspension of two liquids.
- Temporary emulsions separate on standing, whereas permanent emulsions do not.
- **Homogenization** is the formation of a permanent emulsion.
- Emulsifying agents are substances that prevent an emulsion from separating.

Lesson 6-4

- A **colloid** is a suspension in which the particles are permanently suspended.
- The particles of a colloid are larger than the particles of a solution but smaller than those of an ordinary suspension.
- The particles of a colloid are kept in suspension because they are always colliding with the molecules around them.

Lesson 6-5

- **Pollution** is the release of harmful substances into the environment.
- Most pollution is caused by human activities.
- Air pollution is harmful to people.
- Everyone can help to reduce air pollution.
- **Potable water** is safe to drink.

Key Term Challenges

coagulation (p. 132)
colloid (p. 136)
emulsion (p. 134)
filtration (p. 132)
homogenization (p. 134)
pollution (p. 140)
potable water (p. 140)
suspension (p. 130)

MATCHING Write the Key Term from above that best matches each description.

1. water that is safe to drink
2. making the particles in a suspension clump together
3. formation of a permanent emulsion
4. suspension in which particles are permanently suspended
5. release of harmful substances into the environment
6. suspension of two liquids

FILL IN Write the Key Term from above that best completes each statement.

7. A _____ is a cloudy mixture of two or more substances that settles on standing.
8. Passing a suspension through paper or other substances is called _____.
9. A suspension of two liquids is called an _____.
10. Particles in a suspension are clumped together by the process of _____.

Content Challenges TEST PREP

MULTIPLE CHOICE Write the letter of the term or phrase that best completes each statement.

1. If a suspension of clay, sand, and gravel is allowed to stand, the particles that settle out first would be
   a. clay.
   b. sand.
   c. gravel.
   d. water.

2. Colloids cannot be separated by filtration because colloid particles are
   a. round.
   b. too large.
   c. too small.
   d. clumped together.

3. A process that speeds up the separation of a suspension is
   a. homogenization.
   b. pollution.
   c. emulsification.
   d. coagulation.

4. An example of an emulsifying agent is
   a. milk.
   b. egg yolk.
   c. fog.
   d. oil and water.

5. A device that separates a suspension by spinning is called a
   a. centrifuge.
   b. homogenizer.
   c. filter.
   d. coagulator.

6. Both colloids and suspensions
   a. have large particles.
   b. are clear.
   c. scatter light.
   d. settle on standing.

7. The particles in a colloid are
   a. smaller than in a solution.
   b. smaller than in a suspension.
   c. smaller than molecules.
   d. larger than in a suspension.

8. An emulsifying agent makes an emulsion that is
   a. temporary.
   b. liquid.
   c. permanent.
   d. soapy.

9. All of the following are colloids except
   a. fog.
   b. salad dressing.
   c. smoke.
   d. whipped cream.

10. Settling, coagulation, and filtration are examples of
    a. suspensions.
    b. emulsifying agents.
    c. homogenization.
    d. separation methods.

TRUE/FALSE Write *true* if the statement is true. If the statement is false, change the underlined term to make the statement true.

11. Light is scattered by particles in a <u>suspension</u>.

12. Unhomogenized milk is a <u>temporary</u> suspension.

13. When a suspension is left standing, the <u>larger</u> particles are the last to settle.

14. Solutions, colloids, and suspensions are all <u>mixtures</u>.

15. An emulsion is a suspension of two <u>gases</u>.

Concept Challenges TEST PREP

WRITTEN RESPONSE Complete the exercises and answer each of the following questions in complete sentences.

1. EXPLAIN: How does an emulsifying agent work?

2. CONTRAST: In what ways do colloids differ from ordinary suspensions?

3. EXPLAIN: How does the constant motion of colloid particles affect the properties of a colloid?

4. EXPLAIN: How could you test a mixture to find out if it is a solution, a suspension, or a colloid?

INTERPRETING A VISUAL Use Figure 6-17 to answer the following questions.

5. What sources of air pollution are shown in the picture?

6. What sources of water pollution are shown?

7. Which pollutants are gases? Which are liquids? Which are solids?

8. How could each source of air pollution be reduced?

9. Would you expect to find healthy fish and plants in the lake? Why or why not?

10. A rural area 20 km from the area shown in this picture has no factories or other industry. However, the town's water supply is polluted with chemical wastes. How might this be explained?

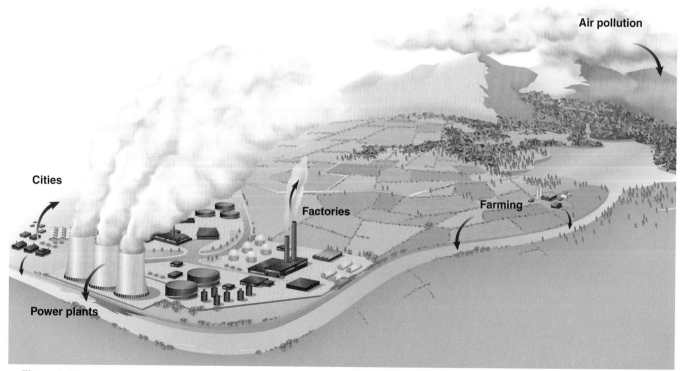

▲ Figure 6-17

Appendix A   Metric System

The Metric System and SI Units

The metric system is an international system of measurement based on units of ten. More than 90% of the nations of the world use the metric system. In the United States, both the English system and the metric system are used.

The *Système International*, or SI, has been used as the international measurement system since 1960. The SI is a modernized version of the metric system. Like the metric system, the SI is a decimal system based on units of ten. When you want to change from one unit in the metric system to another unit, you multiply or divide by a multiple of ten.

- When you change from a smaller unit to a larger unit, you divide.

- When you change from a larger unit to a smaller unit, you multiply.

METRIC UNITS

LENGTH	SYMBOL	RELATIONSHIP
kilometer	km	1 km = 1,000 m
meter	m	1 m = 100 cm
centimeter	cm	1 cm = 10 mm
millimeter	mm	1 mm = 0.1 cm
AREA	**SYMBOL**	
square kilometer	km^2	$1\ km^2 = 1{,}000{,}000\ m^2$
square meter	m^2	$1\ m^2 = 1{,}000{,}000\ mm^2$
square centimeter	cm^2	$1\ cm^2 = 0.0001\ m^2$
square millimeter	mm^2	$1\ mm^2 = 0.000001\ m^2$
VOLUME	**SYMBOL**	
cubic meter	m^3	$1\ m^3 = 1{,}000{,}000\ cm^3$
cubic centimeter	cm^3	$1\ cm^3 = 0.000001\ m^3$
liter	L	1 L = 1,000 mL
milliliter	mL	1 mL = 0.001 L
MASS	**SYMBOL**	
metric ton	t	1 t = 1,000 kg
kilogram	kg	1 kg = 1,000 g
gram	g	1 g = 1,000 mg
centigram	cg	1 cg = 10 mg
milligram	mg	1 mg = 0.001 g
TEMPERATURE	**SYMBOL**	
Kelvin	K	
degree Celsius	°C	

▲ Figure 1

COMMON METRIC PREFIXES

micro-	0.000001 or 1/1,000,000	deka-	10
milli-	0.001 or 1/1,000	hecto-	100
centi-	0.01 or 1/100	kilo-	1,000
deci-	0.1 or 1/10	mega-	1,000,000

▲ Figure 2

METRIC-STANDARD EQUIVALENTS

SI to English	English to SI
LENGTH	
1 kilometer = 0.621 mile (mi)	1 mi = 1.61 km
1 meter = 1.094 yards (yd)	1 yd = 0.914 m
1 meter = 3.28 feet (ft)	1 ft = 0.305 m
1 centimeter = 0.394 inch (in.)	1 in. = 2.54 cm
1 millimeter = 0.039 inch	1 in. = 25.4 mm
AREA	
1 square kilometer = 0.3861 square mile	$1\ mi^2 = 2.590\ km^2$
1 square meter = 1.1960 square yards	$1\ yd^2 = 0.8361\ m^2$
1 square meter = 10.763 square feet	$1\ ft^2 = 0.0929\ m^2$
1 square centimeter = 0.155 square inch	$1\ in.^2 = 6.452\ cm^2$
VOLUME	
1 cubic meter = 1.3080 cubic yards	$1\ yd^3 = 0.7646\ m^3$
1 cubic meter = 35.315 cubic feet	$1\ ft^3 = 0.0283\ m^3$
1 cubic centimeter = 0.0610 cubic inch	$1\ in.^3 = 16.39\ cm^3$
1 liter = 0.2642 gallon (gal)	1 gal = 3.79 L
1 liter = 1.06 quarts (qt)	1 qt = 0.946 L
1 liter = 2.11 pints (pt)	1 pt = 0.47 L
1 milliliter = 0.034 fluid ounce (fl oz)	1 fl oz = 29.57 mL
MASS	
1 metric ton = 0.984 ton	1 ton = 1.016 t
1 kilogram = 2.205 pounds (lb)	1 lb = 0.4536 kg
1 gram = 0.0353 ounce (oz)	1 oz = 28.35 g
TEMPERATURE	
Celsius = 5/9(°F − 32)	Fahrenheit = 9/5°C + 32
0°C = 32°F (Freezing point of water)	72°F = 22°C (Room temperature)
100°C = 212°F (Boiling point of water)	98.6°F = 37°C (Human body temperature)
Kelvin = (°F + 459.67)/1.8	Fahrenheit = (K × 1.8) − 459.67

▲ Figure 3

Appendix B Chemical Elements

LIST OF CHEMICAL ELEMENTS		
Element	Atomic Symbol	Atomic Number
Actinium	Ac	89
Aluminum	Al	13
Americium	Am	95
Antimony	Sb	51
Argon	Ar	18
Arsenic	As	33
Astatine	At	85
Barium	Ba	56
Berkelium	Bk	97
Beryllium	Be	4
Bismuth	Bi	83
Bohrium	Bh	107
Boron	B	5
Bromine	Br	35
Cadmium	Cd	48
Calcium	Ca	20
Californium	Cf	98
Carbon	C	6
Cerium	Ce	58
Cesium	Cs	55
Chlorine	Cl	17
Chromium	Cr	24
Cobalt	Co	27
Copper	Cu	29
Curium	Cm	96
Dubnium	Db	105
Dysprosium	Dy	66
Einsteinium	Es	99
Erbium	Er	68
Europium	Eu	63
Fermium	Fm	100
Fluorine	F	9
Francium	Fr	87
Gadolinium	Gd	64
Gallium	Ga	31
Germanium	Ge	32
Gold	Au	79

▲ Figure 4

LIST OF CHEMICAL ELEMENTS		
Element	Atomic Symbol	Atomic Number
Hafnium	Hf	72
Hassium	Hs	108
Helium	He	2
Holmium	Ho	67
Hydrogen	H	1
Indium	In	49
Iodine	I	53
Iridium	Ir	77
Iron	Fe	26
Krypton	Kr	36
Lanthanum	La	57
Lawrencium	Lr	103
Lead	Pb	82
Lithium	Li	3
Lutetium	Lu	71
Magnesium	Mg	12
Manganese	Mn	25
Meitnerium	Mt	109
Mendelevium	Md	101
Mercury	Hg	80
Molybdenum	Mo	42
Neodymium	Nd	60
Neon	Ne	10
Neptunium	Np	93
Nickel	Ni	28
Niobium	Nb	41
Nitrogen	N	7
Nobelium	No	102
Osmium	Os	76
Oxygen	O	8
Palladium	Pd	46
Phosphorus	P	15
Platinum	Pt	78
Plutonium	Pu	94
Polonium	Po	84
Potassium	K	19
Praseodymium	Pr	59
Promethium	Pm	61

LIST OF CHEMICAL ELEMENTS		
Element	Atomic Symbol	Atomic Number
Protactinium	Pa	91
Radium	Ra	88
Radon	Rn	86
Rhenium	Re	75
Rhodium	Rh	45
Rubidium	Rb	37
Ruthenium	Ru	44
Rutherfordium	Rf	104
Samarium	Sm	62
Scandium	Sc	21
Seaborgium	Sg	106
Selenium	Se	34
Silicon	Si	14
Silver	Ag	47
Sodium	Na	11
Strontium	Sr	38
Sulfur	S	16
Tantalum	Ta	73
Technetium	Tc	43
Tellurium	Te	52
Terbium	Tb	65
Thallium	Tl	81
Thorium	Th	90
Thulium	Tm	69
Tin	Sn	50
Titanium	Ti	22
Tungsten	W	74
Ununnilium	Uun	110
Unununium	Uuu	111
Ununbium	Uub	112
Ununquadium	Uuq	114
Uranium	U	92
Vanadium	V	23
Xenon	Xe	54
Ytterbium	Yb	70
Yttrium	Y	39
Zinc	Zn	30
Zirconium	Zr	40

Appendix C Science Terms

Analyzing Science Terms

You can often unlock the meaning of an unfamiliar science term by analyzing its word parts. Prefixes and suffixes, for example, each carry a meaning that comes from a word root. This word root usually comes from the Latin or Greek language. The following list of prefixes and suffixes provides clues to the meaning of many science terms.

WORD PART	MEANING	EXAMPLE
-ate	salt of an acid	nitrate
bar-, baro-	weight, pressure	barometer
bi-	two	binary
carbo-	containing carbon	carbonate
co-	with, together	coagulation
de-	remove from	decomposition
electro-	electricity	electrolyte
-graph	write	thermograph
hydro-	water, containing hydrogen	hydrometer, hydrocarbon
-ide	binary compound	sulfide
in-	not	insoluble
-logy	study of	cosmology
-lysis	decomposition	electrolysis
magneto-	magnetism	magnetosphere
-meter	measuring device	manometer
non-	not	nonmetal
photo-	light	photoelectric
poly-	many	polyatomic
re-	again, back	reflection
-sonic	sound	supersonic
-sphere	ball, globe	magnetosphere
sub-	under, beneath	subscript
super-	above, more than	supersonic
therm-, thermo-	heat	thermometer
trans-	across, beyond	transparent
ultra-	beyond	ultrasound
un-	not	unsaturated

▲ Figure 5

Appendix D Mathematics Review

Adding Integers

You can add integers with unlike signs on a number line.

Add $^-5 + {}^+7$

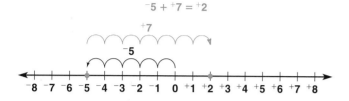

Subtracting Integers

To subtract an integer, add its opposite.

Subtract $^-6 - {}^+2$

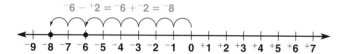

Multiplying Integers

When you multiply integers, you must decide if the answer is positive or negative.

If the signs of the integers are the same, the product is positive.

$$^+5 \times {}^+4 = {}^+20$$
$$^-5 \times {}^-4 = {}^+20$$

If the signs of the integers are different, the product is negative.

$$^+5 \times {}^-4 = {}^-20$$
$$^-5 \times {}^+4 = {}^-20$$

Dividing Integers

The rules for dividing integers are the same as the rules for multiplying integers.

If the signs of the integers are the same, the quotient is positive.

$$^-36 \div {}^-9 = {}^+4$$
$$^+36 \div {}^+9 = {}^+4$$

If the signs of the integers are different, the quotient is negative.

$$^-36 \div {}^+9 = {}^-4$$
$$^+36 \div {}^-9 = {}^-4$$

Solving an Equation

To solve an equation, find the value of the variable that makes the equation true.

Is $b = 3$ the solution to the equation?

$$4b = 12$$

Replace b with 3 in the equation.

$$4 \times 3 = 12$$
$$12 = 12$$

Yes, $b = 3$ is the solution to the equation.

Adding and Subtracting Decimals

When adding or subtracting decimals, always be sure to line up the decimal points correctly.

Add 3.4 km, 20.95 km, and 153.6 km.

```
    3.4
   20.95
+ 153.6
 177.95 km
```

Subtract 13.5 mL from 35.75 mL.

```
  35.75
- 13.5
  22.25 mL
```

Multiplying and Dividing Decimals

When multiplying or dividing decimals, it is not necessary to line up the decimal points.

Multiply 0.5 N by 11.25 m to find the amount of work done in joules.

$$W = F \times d$$

$$W = 0.5 \text{ N} \times 11.25 \text{ m}$$

$$W = 5.625 \text{ J}$$

Notice that the number of places to the right of the decimal point in the answer is equal to the sum of the places to the right of the decimal point in the numbers being multiplied.

Divide 4.05 m by 0.5 m to find the mechanical advantage of a lever.

$$MA = \text{effort arm length/resistance arm length}$$

$$MA = 4.05 \text{ m}/0.5 \text{ m}$$

$$MA = 8.1$$

When dividing a decimal by another decimal, you must first change the divisor to a whole number. For example, change 0.5 to 5 by moving the decimal point one place to the right. You must also change the dividend by moving the decimal point one place to the right. The result is $40.5 \div 5 = 8.1$.

Changing a Decimal to a Percent

To change a decimal to a percent, multiply the decimal by 100%.

Find the efficiency of a machine if the work output is 5 J and the work input is 10 J.

Efficiency = work output ÷ work input × 100%

Efficiency = 5 J ÷ 10 J × 100%

Efficiency = 0.5 × 100%

Efficiency = 50%

Notice that when you multiply 0.5 by 100%, the decimal point moves two places to the right.

Measuring Angles

Use a protractor to measure an angle. Place the center of the protractor's straight edge on the vertex. One ray must pass through 0°.

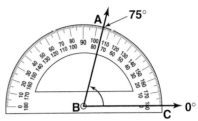

Angle ABC measures 75°.

Solving Word Problems

To solve distance problems, you can use $d = r \times t$ or $d = rt$.

The Smiths drove 220 miles at an average speed of 55 miles per hour. How long did the trip take?

PLAN

Substitute the values you know into the equation $d = r \times t$.

Then solve.

DO

$$220 = 55t$$

$$220 \div 55 = 55t \div 55$$

$$4 = t$$

SOLUTION

The trip took 4 hours.

Glossary

Pronunciation and syllabication have been derived from *Webster's New World Dictionary*, Second College Edition, Revised School Printing (Prentice Hall, 1985). Syllables printed in capital letters are given primary stress. (Numbers in parentheses indicate the page number, or page numbers, on which the term is defined.)

Symbol	Example	Respelling	Symbol	Example	Respelling
a	transverse	(trans-VURS)	oh	coagulation	(koh-ag-yoo-LAY-shuhn)
ah	velocity	(vuh-LAHS-uh-tee)	oo	amplitude	(AM-pluh-tood)
aw	trough	(TRAWF)	oi	colloid	(KAHL-oid)
ay	radiation	(ray-dee-AY-shuhn)	s	solute	(SAHL-yoot)
eh	convection	(kuhn-VEHK-shuhn)	sh	suspension	(suh-SPEHN-shuhn)
ee	decomposition	(dee-kahm-puh-ZIH-shuhn)	u	fulcrum	(FOOL-kruhm)
f	coefficient	(koh-uh-FIHSH-uhnt)	uh	barometer	(buh-RAHM-uht-uhr)
ih	specialization	(spehsh-uhl-ih-ZAY-shuhn)	y, eye	binary, ion	(BY-nuh-ree), (EYE-uhn)
j	homogenization	(huh-mahj-uh-nih-ZAY-shuhn)	yoo	insoluble	(ihn-SAHL-yoo-buhl)
k	calorie	(KAL-uh-ree)	z	ionization	(eye-uh-nih-ZAY-shuhn)

A

amino acids: building blocks of proteins (p. 96)

atom: smallest part of an element that can be identified as that element (p. 54)

atomic mass: total mass of the protons and neutrons in an atom, measured in atomic mass units (amu) (p. 60)

atomic number: number of protons in the nucleus of an atom (p. 58)

B

boiling point: temperature at which a liquid changes to a gas (p. 116)

boiling point elevation: increase in the boiling point of a liquid solvent because of the addition of a solute (p. 116)

buoyancy (BOI-uhn-see): tendency of an object to float in a fluid (p. 44)

C

carbohydrates (kahr-boh-HY-drayts): sugars and starches (p. 96)

chemical bond: force of attraction that holds atoms together (p. 82)

chemical change: change that produces new substances (p. 26)

chemical symbol: shortened way of writing the name of an element (p. 64)

chemistry (KEHM-ihs-tree): branch of science that deals with the study of the structure and the makeup of matter and the changes matter undergoes (p. 16)

coagulation (koh-ag-yoo-LAY-shuhn): use of chemicals to make the particles in a suspension clump together (p. 132)

colloid (KAHL-oid): suspension in which the particles are permanently suspended (p. 136)

communication: sharing information (p. 8)

compound: substance made up of two or more elements that are chemically combined (p. 80)

concentrated solution: solution containing a large amount of solute compared with the amount of solvent present (p. 112)

condensation (kahn-duhn-SAY-shuhn): change from a gas to a liquid (pp. 22, 118)

constant: something that does not change (p. 11)

controlled experiment: experiment in which all the conditions except one are kept constant (p. 11)

covalent bond: bond formed when atoms share electrons (p. 92)

D

data: information you collect when you observe something (p. 3)

density (DEHN-suh-tee): mass per unit volume (p. 34)

dilute solution: solution containing a small amount of solute compared with the amount of solvent present (p. 112)

displacement (dihs-PLAYS-muhnt): the replacement, or pushing aside, of a volume of water, or any fluid, by an object (p. 40)

dissolve (dih-ZAHLV): go into solution (p. 104)

distillation (dihs-tuh-LAY-shuhn): process of evaporating a liquid and then condensing the gas back into a liquid (p. 118)

ductile (DUK-tuhl): able to be drawn into thin wires (p. 68)

E

electron: particle that has a negative charge (p. 56)

element (EHL-uh-muhnt): substance that cannot be chemically broken down into simpler substances (pp. 52, 80)

emulsion (ee-MUL-shuhn): suspension of two liquids (p. 134)

energy level: place in an electron cloud where an electron is most likely to be found (p. 62)

evaporation (ee-vap-uh-RAY-shuhn): change from a liquid to a gas at the surface of the liquid (pp. 22, 118)

F

filtration: separation of particles in a suspension by passing the suspension through filter paper or some other porous material (p. 132)

freezing: change from a liquid to a solid (p. 22)

freezing point: temperature at which a liquid changes to a solid (p. 114)

freezing point depression: decrease in the freezing point of a liquid solvent because of the addition of a solute (p. 114)

G

gas: state of matter that has no definite shape or volume (p. 20)

gram: basic unit of mass (p. 4)

group: vertical column of elements in the periodic table (p. 64)

H

halogens: elements that make up Group 17 in the periodic table (p. 70)

homogenization (huh-mahj-uh-nih-ZAY-shuhn): formation of a permanent emulsion (p. 134)

hydrometer (hy-DRAHM-uht-uhr): device used to measure specific gravity (p. 38)

hypothesis: suggested answer to a question or problem (p. 10)

I

insoluble (ihn-SAHL-yoo-buhl): not able to dissolve (p. 106)

ion (EYE-uhn): atom with an electrical charge (p. 90)

ionic bond: bond formed between atoms that have gained or lost electrons (p. 90)

isotope (EYE-suh-tohp): atom of an element with the same number of protons as the other atoms but a different number of neutrons (p. 72)

L

lipids: fats and oils (p. 96)

liquid: state of matter with a definite volume but no definite shape (p. 20)

liter: basic unit of liquid volume (p. 4)

luster (LUS-tuhr): the way a material reflects light (p. 68)

M

malleable (MAL-ee-uh-buhl): able to be hammered into different shapes (p. 68)

mass: amount of matter in something (p. 4)

mass number: number of protons and neutrons in the nucleus of an atom (p. 60)

matter: anything that has mass and takes up space (p. 18)

melting: change from a solid to a liquid (p. 22)

meniscus: curve at the surface of a liquid in a thin tube (p. 4)

meter: basic unit of length or distance (p. 4)

metal: element that has the property of shiny luster, ductility, and malleability (p. 68)

mixture: two or more substances that have been physically combined (p. 80)

model: tool scientists use to represent an object or a process (p. 3)

molecule: smallest part of a substance that has all the properties of that substance (p. 82)

neutron: particle that has no charge (p. 56)

newton: SI unit of force (p. 44)

noble gases: elements that make up Group 18 in the periodic table (p. 70)

nonmetal: element that lacks most of the properties of a metal (p. 68)

nucleic acids: compounds made up of carbon, oxygen, hydrogen, nitrogen, and phosphorus (p. 96)

nucleus: center, or core, of an atom (p. 56)

organic chemistry: study of organic compounds (p. 94)

organic compound: compound containing carbon (p. 94)

period: horizontal row of elements in the periodic table (p. 64)

periodic (pihr-ee-AHD-ihk): repeating pattern (p. 64)

physical change: change that does not produce new substances (p. 26)

physics: branch of science that deals with energy and matter and how they interact (p. 16)

plasma (PLAZ-muh): state of matter made up of electronically charged particles (p. 20)

polar molecule: molecule in which one end has a positive charge and the other end has a negative charge (p. 108)

pollution (puh-LOO-shuhn): release of harmful substances into the environment (p. 140)

polymers: large molecules that are formed by many smaller molecules (p. 94)

potable (POHT-uh-buhl) **water:** water that is safe to drink (p. 140)

properties (PRAHP-uhr-teez): characteristics used to describe an object (p. 18)

proteins: compounds used to build and repair body tissues (p. 96)

proton: particle that has a positive charge (p. 56)

saturated solution: solution containing all the solute it can hold at a given temperature (p. 112)

simulation: computer model that usually shows a process (p. 3)

solid: state of matter with a definite shape and volume (p. 20)

solubility: maximum amount of a substance that will dissolve in a given quantity of a solvent at a given temperature (p. 106)

soluble (SAHL-yoo-buhl): able to dissolve (p. 106)

solute (SAHL-yoot): substance that is dissolved in a solvent (p. 106)

solution: mixture in which the particles of one substance are evenly mixed with the particles of another substance (p. 104)

solvent: substance in which a solute dissolves (p. 106)

specialization (spehsh-uh-lih-ZAY-shuhn): studying or working in one area of a subject (p. 16)

specific (spuh-SIF-ik) **gravity:** density of a substance compared with the density of water (p. 38)

state of matter: any of the four physical forms of matter (p. 20)

structural formula: molecular model that uses straight lines to indicate bonds (p. 94)

sublimation: change from a solid directly to a gas (p. 22)

substance: any element or compound (p. 80)

supersaturated solution: solution containing more solute than it can normally hold at a given temperature (p. 112)

suspension (suh-SPEHN-shuhn): mixture of two or more materials that separate on standing (p. 130)

T

temperature: measurement of the amount of heat energy something contains (p. 4)

theory: set of hypotheses that have been supported by testing over and over again (p. 10)

U

unit: amount used to measure something (p. 4)

unsaturated solution: solution containing less solute than it can hold at a given temperature (p. 112)

V

valence electron: electron in the outermost energy level of an atom (p. 90)

variable: anything that can affect the outcome of an experiment (p. 11)

volume: amount of space an object takes up (p. 4)

Index

experimentation,
scientific method of,
81
extensive properties, 81

F

fats, 96
feldspar, 87
filtering, 85
filtration, 132, 140
fish, in Arctic Ocean,
115
floating, 45
fluorine, 70
fluorine-123, 73
fog, 23, 136
fog machines, 23
food pyramid, 97
foods. *See also* diet.
colloids in, 138–139
emulsions in, 138–139
suspensions in,
138–139
forces, of attraction, 108
formulas, structural,
94–95
fossil fuels, burning,
140
fractional distillation of
petroleum, 119
fractionating tower, 119
freezing, 22
freezing point
effect of solutes on,
114–115
of water, 114
freezing point
depression, 114–115
Fung, Sherman K. W.,
105

G

gallium-67, 73
gases, 20, 68, 104
inert, 70
Gell-Mann, Murray, 57
glass, stained, 129
gold, 51–52, 58, 68, 80, 87
grams per cubic
centimeter, 34, 36
grams per milliliter, 34,
36
granite, 79, 87
gravity, specific, 38–39
groups, 65, 67

H

halogens, 70
hard water, 105
helium, 35, 52, 58, 62, 65,
70–71, 90
Hindenberg disaster, 71

homogenization, 134
hydrogen, 35, 52–53, 58,
65, 68, 80, 82, 87, 90, 92,
94, 96
hydrogen peroxide, 82
hydrogen-1, 72
hydrogen-2, 72
hydrogen-3, 72
hydrometers, 38

I

ice, 20
dry, 23
inert gases, 70
inorganic compounds,
94
insoluble substances,
106–107
intensive properties, 81
iodine, 70
iodine-123, 73
ionic bonds, 90–93
ionic compounds, 91–92
comparing covalent
compounds and, 92
ionic solutions, 109
ions, 90
iron, 34, 52, 86, 87, 105
iron sulfide, 86–87
isomers, 95
isotopes, 72
of common elements,
72–73
radioactive, 73

K

kilogram, 19, 34
krypton, 70
kryptonite, 70

L

lattice
in crystals, 114
Lavoisier, Antoine, 19
Lavoisier, Marie Anne,
19
law of conservation of
mass, 19
lead, 34, 52, 64
Lee, Tsung Dao, 59
leptons, 57
limestone, 107
lipids, 96
liquids, 20, 68, 104
density of, 36–37
liquid solutions, 104
lithium, 60, 62, 65
living things, need for
organic compounds,
96–97
luster, 68

M

magnesium, 105
magnesium chloride,
114
magnets, 86
malleable, 68
mantle, 21
mass, 18, 19, 34, 42, 60
mass number, 60
matter, 18
chemical changes in,
26, 28–29
elements and, 52–53
physical changes in,
26–29
properties of, 18, 26,
42–43
states of, 15, 20–21
changes in, 22, 24–25
studying, 19
types of, 80–81
mechanical weathering,
107
melting, 22
Mendeleev, Dmitri, 61,
64
mercury, 34, 52, 68
metals, 68
comparing nonmetals
and, 69
properties of, 68
mica, 87
microscope, 130
milliliter, 34, 36
mineralogists, 39, 91
minerals, 39
Mississippi delta, 133
mixtures, 79–102
comparing compounds
and, 86–87
kinds of, 84
making, 86
separating, 84–85,
88–89
molecular model, 93
molecular solutions, 108
molecules, 82, 98, 111
polar, 108
water, 108
monomers, 95
motion, Brownian, 137

N

neon, 52, 58, 70, 71
neutral atoms, 90
neutron star, 35
neutrons, 56, 57, 60–61,
74
newtons, 44
nickel, 52
nitrogen, 68, 96, 97, 105,
106

Nobel Prize, 53
noble gases, 70–71
nonmetals, 68
comparing metals and,
69
properties of, 68
nonpolar molecules, 111
nuclear energy, 16
nuclear physics, 16
nuclear power plants,
140
nuclei, 56, 74
nucleic acids, 96–97
nucleus, 56

O

oils, 96, 134
optical crystals, 122
optics, 16
organic chemistry, 94
organic compounds,
94–95
need of living things
for, 96–97
oxygen, 52–53, 58, 68, 80,
82, 86, 87, 92, 94, 96,
105–106, 110

P

particle accelerators, 55,
57
periodic table, 64–65, 72
of elements, 66–67
periods, 65, 67
permanent emulsions,
134
petroleum, fractional
distillation of, 119
phosphorus, 68, 97
physical changes, 26–29
observing, 27
physical properties, 26,
85, 95
of water, 85
physical science
importance of, 16
specialized fields in, 16
studying, 16
physical scientists,
16–17
physicists, 59
physics, 16
plants, 98
plasma, 21
plastic state, 21
plastics, 94
poisonous compounds,
98–99
poisonous substances,
98
polar molecules, 108
polar solvents, 111
pollutants, in air, 141

Photo Credits